Modern Graphic Arts
Paste-Up

Gerald A. Silver, Ed. D.—Faculty, Los Angeles City College; Owner, Literary Graphics, North Hollywood, California.

VNR VAN NOSTRAND REINHOLD COMPANY
NEW YORK CINCINNATI TORONTO LONDON MELBOURNE

First published in paperback in 1983.

Copyright © 1966, 1973, by American Technical Publishers, Inc.

Library of Congress Catalog Card Number: 82-50746
ISBN: 0-442-28166-8

Printed in The United States of America.

Van Nostrand Reinhold Company Inc.
135 West 50th Street, New York, NY 10020

First published 1966 by American Technical Publishers, Inc.
Twelfth Printing 1982

16   15   14   13   12   11   10   9   8   7   6   5   4   3   2   1

Table of Contents

Preface to the Second Edition

The Graphic Arts industry continues to grow—more than one billion dollars are paid out annually in salaries. Gross receipts in the Graphic Arts climb at the rate of more than 350 million dollars a year. The need for persons skilled in Graphic Arts techniques grows with the industry. *Modern Graphic Arts Paste-Up* opens the door to a dynamic industry.

Job opportunities in the preparation of material for the Graphic Arts camera increase daily. Not only are more and more newspapers—daily and weekly—"going offset," but many letterpress publications find it economical to paste-up display and advertising pages using cold type methods. Design flexibility is a key feature of paste-up. This flexibility is particularly suitable to supermarket and drugstore advertisements. Business publications, technical reports, magazines and many others use camera copy preparation techniques. Gravure and screen process printing are also photographic processes requiring this kind of preparation.

The second edition of *Modern Graphic Arts Paste-Up* introduces the student to practices as well as the scope of the Graphic Arts industry. This laboratory manual explores the techniques of paste-up work. Elementary Graphic Arts instruction has too long been tied solely to hand composition. *Modern Graphic Arts Paste-Up* includes, but goes beyond, hand composition. This workbook explores areas that are only possible because of the flexibility of using a paste-up as the center of each lesson. The lessons each focus on a single concept or practice in paste-up work. By using the paste-up as the core of instruction, the student has both a record of his progress and tangible evidence of his achievement. The completed projects may also serve to prod the student to further study or practice.

In this second edition, the first chapter has been expanded to include material on adhesive lettering. An entirely new chapter on basic principles of layout has been added, as well as three new units on the IBM "Selectric" Composer, adhesive tapes, and newspaper display advertisement.

Most lessons also provide exploratory exercises for the advanced student. The exercises are intended to allow the student to explore paste-up techniques further. Although they are designed *into* the program of instruction provided by the "regular" lessons, the exploratory exercises allow the student to go *beyond* the single concept already explored.

"We learn by doing" has been so often repeated that it has become a cliche—but it is still a useful educational concept. This laboratory manual is geared to that concept.

Finally, the lessons and the exploratory exercises will provide the student with a portfolio of his work. This portfolio will be useful to him in seeking work. From this initial opportunity, he can make his way in one of many directions to even higher wages and greater personal satisfaction.

A Paste-Up Centered Introduction to Graphic Arts

Since the turn of the century, elementary education in Graphic Arts has followed a familiar pattern. The fundamental learning experiences are centered on hand composition. Usually the student sets small blocks of copy, pulls proofs, distributes his type, and receives a grade. Through this process he is introduced to hanging indentions, inverted pyramids, justified lines, etc.

This approach has its weaknesses. Many feel that setting type is tedious and unmotivating and fails to open the students' minds and eyes to the dynamics and vitality of the printing industry. The logistics of assigning type cases and spacing material to large numbers of students presents a real problem, especially during the hectic opening weeks of the semester. Elaborate schemes, including meticulous character counts of the type case have detracted from the learning experience. Creativity and individual artistic ability may find little expression in hand composition approaches. Photocomposing, strike-on composition and adhesive lettering are widely used in the industry, and further undermine the validity of teaching hand composition to massive numbers of students.

Few can deny the inroads that offset has made into letterpress printing. Offset has brought about a need for a new and more realistic instructional technique in Graphic Arts. Changing employment demands are markedly affecting the preparation young people need to enter the Graphic Arts.

The paste-up is an effective introduction to Graphic Arts, from the junior high school through the junior college and technical school. It can teach most skills learned in hand composition, plus a great deal more. It stimulates interest and creativity and exposes the student to a variety of Graphic Arts theories. An introductory program should center on a series of progressive paste-ups. The student executes these at his desk, with simple tools. They are graded on cleanliness, accuracy, mechanical requirements, adherence to instructions and artistic and creative effort.

Each paste-up should teach a fundamental Graphic Arts theory or principle. Paste-ups can explore type size, point system, proofreaders' marks, layout and design, use of the ruling pen, tint screens, register marks, overlays, handling photographs, multi-color printing, etc. The list is limited only by the creativity of the instructor. He is not confined to what can be set in the type stick. The student is free to use many resources for artwork and ideas.

The paste-up centered learning experience is a valuable tool in the hands of the student and the teacher:

1. The collection of exercises provides an excellent review before examinations and quizzes.

2. It is a compendium of resources and ideas available to the student after completing the course.
3. It is a job portfolio, graphically illustrating the student's abilities.
4. It teaches a salable job skill.
5. It is a tangible, creative exercise which may be taken home.
6. It provides the instructor with an objective means of grading.
7. It may be employed with a minimum amount of equipment and space.

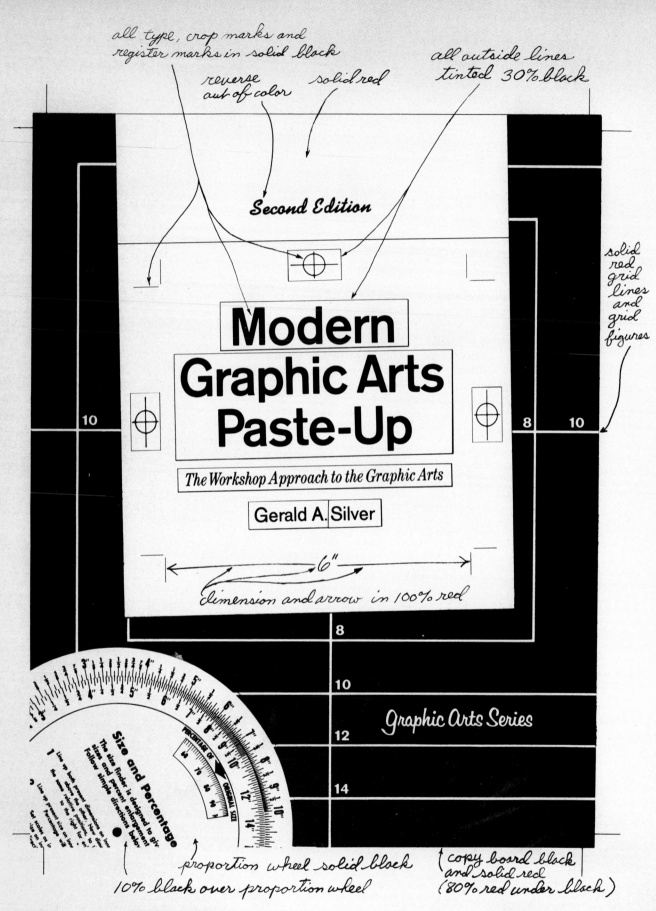

Graphic Arts
Paste-Up

What Is a Paste-Up?

A paste-up is a combination of type that has been set and proofed, drawings, hand lettering and illustrations designed to be photographically copied and reproduced as a printed page.

Paste-ups are used for a variety of purposes in different types of printing. They are particularly important in the lithographic process which requires camera-ready copy. The function of the paste-up is to collect all the various items (text and art work) that make up the finished product.

All paste-ups are created for a single purpose—to be photographed. There are some rules and procedures which will improve the end product. This book reviews many of these. In some instances, low printing quality may be traced directly to the early stages of paste-up. Poor techniques, poor original copy or lack of planning—all lead to low quality printing.

Paste-Up and the Offset Process

A brief review will show the relationship of paste-up to the finished product. The printing designer is first supplied with copy and illustrations. He must also know the objective of the final product. He studies these (copy, illustrations and objective) as well as the presses available, costs and other factors. With this information, he designs the job, creating thumbnail, rough and comprehensive layouts. These layouts help in visualizing the completed printing job.

After the final layout has been approved, paste-up work begins. All elements of copy, simple line drawings, photographs and text, are combined by the paste-up artist into a single unit. Instructions on color of ink, type of paper, and other necessary details are written. The paste-up and specifications are then sent to the lithographer.

Here all elements of the paste-up are photographed. Line copy[1] is grouped and photographed as a unit. Halftone[2] copy is photographed separately.

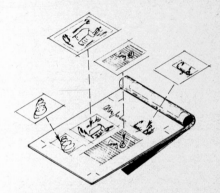

Paste-up

---

1. *Line copy*—Copy has two meanings in the graphic arts. It means words or writing for a printing job. It also means the complete job to be photographed. In this book it will always mean the latter. Line copy is any matter that is to be photographed without gradations of color. The text on this page is line copy.

2. *Halftone copy*—All material that has continuous shades of gray must be broken up into a pattern of black and white dots so that it will appear to have gray tones. Photographs are treated in this way. Halftone copy must be photographed separately through a screen which breaks up the continuous tone of the original art into discrete areas of black and white.

Halftone reproduction

1

Next, a complete set of negatives is sent to the stripper.[3] Negatives are taped to large sheets of masking paper, each in a predetermined position. Halftone and color separation negatives are combined at this point. Openings are cut into the masking sheets to expose areas which contain an image. Imperfections in the negatives are opaqued[4] out by hand. A small brush and a light-opaque paint are used.

After stripping, the completed work goes to the platemaker. Large vacuum frames hold the negatives in direct contact with light sensitive plates. An arc lamp transfers the image on the negatives to the light-sensitive emulsion on the plate. After desensitizing and lacquering, the plates are forwarded to the press room.

The modern lithographic pressroom is equipped with rotary presses. The plates are mounted on cylinders. The press is turned on, causing the cylinders to revolve. As the plate cylinder turns, it contacts the water and ink rollers. The water will not stick to the image areas, because they are coated with an oily lacquer. (Oil and water, of course, will not mix.) Once water is deposited on the plate the ink will only adhere to the image areas. The ink has an oil base, and is attracted to the oily lacquer forming an image.

Next the revolving plate with the ink covered image contacts a blanket (rubber covered cylinder). The image is transferred to the blanket. The blanket transfers the image to the paper as it passes under the blanket.

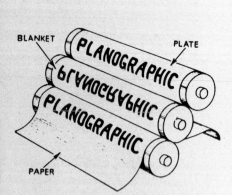

Offset lithography

Paste-Ups and Other Printing Processes

Offset printing utilizes a paste-up because it is the most convenient way to combine the needed elements. However, paste-ups are also convenient in intaglio printing and relief printing (letterpress).

All copy and illustrations are pasted up for high speed rotogravure. First, type is set and reproduction proofs[5] are pulled. They are then pasted up and art work is added. When the paste-up is complete it is photographed.[6] The image from the negative is exposed on a sheet of transfer film. The film is then placed around a smooth cylinder. The image areas are etched to produce wells in the cylinder. These wells hold the ink. As the cylinder revolves through an ink "bath" it picks up ink. A scraper (called a doctor blade) removes the ink from the smooth surface of the cylinder and the ink remains in the wells. When the paper passes under the cylinder, it is pressed into the wells and the image is transferred to the sheet.

Paste-up finds application in letterpress printing. Dycril and other rapid letterpress platemaking methods begin with copy that is pasted-up. Negatives are made and the image is transferred to plates, which are then

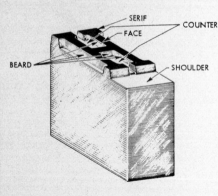

Relief printing

---

3. The *stripper* combines the halftone negative with the line negative and performs the other duties which are explained above. *Stripping* is the combining of halftone and line films. Stripping, of course, must precede the platemaking process.

4. *Opaquing* is the process of painting over any unwanted transparent areas in the negative. These transparent areas, of course, would print as small black specks on the finished job if they were not opaqued out before the plate was made.

5. *Reproduction proofs.* Proofs are the first copies of printed matter made. Reproduction proofs are high quality prints of type, usually made on a small hand press one at a time.

6. *Gravure photography.* The entire gravure print has a dot pattern. Illustrations, pictures, line art and text may be photographed together. Stripping of negatives is unnecessary in gravure printing.

processed to produce a relief image. By working with cold type copy instead of letterpress forms, flexibility is gained. Line drawings and half-tones may be included and reproduced on a single lightweight plate for small additional expense.

Cold type device

Lithographic Film

To take full advantage of the flexibility of cold-type copy preparation, it is important to understand the various types of film, and how they are affected by color.

There are three common Graphic Arts films used in lithography. Each of these films has a particular range of color sensitivity because of the nature of the chemicals used in their manufacture. These sensitivity variables are useful to the lithographer.

Monochromatic Films. These films are coated with a color-blind emulsion. They are used for copying black and white originals. Their narrow range limits their utility.

Orthochromatic Films. These films will copy black and white originals and any copy in red or orange. They will not pick up blue guidelines. Orthochromatic films are normally processed in a darkroom equipped with a *red* safelight. The observer may check the development as it progresses, and stop it when the negative has reached its optimum point. For these reasons, it is the most widely used lithographic film.

Filters may be used with this film. These are thin sheets of gelatin inserted between the lens and copy (or within the waterhouse opening of the lens) which increase the contrast of the copy. Colors may be dropped or accentuated by the proper choice of filters. To hold a given color, the cameraman uses a filter of a complementary hue. To drop a color, a filter of the same hue is used.

Panchromatic Films. When the film emulsion is made sensitive to all colors, it is called panchromatic. It will record all the colors in the visual spectrum as various shades of gray.

Development of this film must be carried on in total darkness. Only at the end of the developing period may a low intensity *green* safelight be used for a short duration. This film is processed at a fixed temperature, for a specific period of time. Normally, no visual observations are made during development, and errors in exposure mean reshooting and reprocessing.

Its sensitivity to a wide range of colors make panchromatic film best suited for color separations. Panchromatic film is also used when copy contains colors which the artist cannot control. Care must be exercised when making a paste-up to be copied with this film, *since blue guidelines will photograph.*

When black is to be used on the paste-up, it must be a dense, even black. Weak, uneven black or gray will not reproduce properly because of the high-contrast nature of orthochromatic and monochromatic films which are used in Graphic Arts, a color is either picked up entirely or dropped entirely. Hand lettering, ruling, and signatures must all be done in dense black ink. India ink is almost always suitable, since it possesses the needed quality density.

When using orthochromatic films, red may be substituted for black. Maximum contrast is obtained between image and non-image areas by using the whitest paper available. The greater the contrast, the greater the latitude and ease in developing the negative.

Basic Paste-Up Tools

Proper tools and an understanding of their use is essential in producing neat and accurate paste-ups. If all necessary tools and materials are at hand before beginning, efficiency and high quality are more likely to result.

Best results are obtained when paste-ups are done on a drawing table adjusted to a comfortable height and properly illuminated. An adjustable chair or stool should be available.

A primary tool used in paste-up work is the drawing board. This board is an accurately manufactured piece of softwood, trimmed square on all sides. It is used to mount a piece of illustration board upon which the paste-up is done. Along with the drawing board, a T square is necessary. Metal or wooden T squares will suffice, provided that they are true. With these, the artist is assured that all proofs and illustrations are parallel.

Fasten three or four strips of acetate or stiff cardboard under each side of the T square. If masking tape is available four strips taped along each edge of the T square will raise it slightly, preventing ink from smearing under it. Three or four pennies or washers, secured with masking tape, will also suffice. Some T squares have raised edges to prevent the ink from smearing.

A plastic 30°-60° triangle may also prove useful. In addition, a 12″ or 18″ photographic print trimmer is helpful when trimming proofs to size.

If many paste-ups are to be done, it is recommended that the craftsman use a drafting machine. This instrument replaces the T square and triangle, and assures parallel lines with greater speed and accuracy than any other method.

Rubber cement is the standard adhesive used in paste-up work. There are several reasons for this. Rubber cement dries clear and is flexible. Proofs may be removed by placing a few drops of white gasoline or rubber cement solvent under the edge. The rubber cement releases its bond making rearrangement of proofs easy. It is also economical and readily available. A low cost grade of rubber cement may turn artwork brown, or even release its hold. For artwork of a more permanent nature, double-coated scotch tape from a suitable dispenser is effective.

Rubber cement is used in two ways. The most rapid is to apply a dab of cement to the back of the proof, square it up and press it down using a sheet of paper over the proof to keep it clean. For a more permanent bond, apply rubber cement to both the proof and the illustration board. Let both dry. Position the proof over the board and press it down using a sheet of paper. The latter, while more permanent, makes the aligning of proofs slightly more difficult.

A newer more satisfactory method of applying proofs is by the use of a wax coating machine. Wax is applied to the back of the proof by the machine. The proof is then pressed into place. It may be easily removed by peeling it off. Wax coaters are available in small hand-held models that deposit a 1″ strip of wax and larger models which coat the entire proof in one pass.

A light blue pencil is used for layout to designate margins, paper and image areas. A sky blue shade should be chosen because it will not reproduce on orthochromatic film. The artist may use any guide, control and alignment lines without the necessity of erasing them—as long as orthochromatic film is used in the camera. As a convenience and time-saver, rely upon these lines as much as possible.

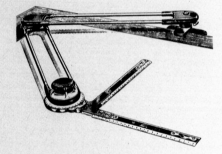

Drafting machine

Wax coating machine

A sharp x-acto knife and scissors are necessary items. Keep both sharp and they will cut accurately with little tearing of the paper fibers. A small sharpening stone is convenient for keeping knife edges sharp.

A ruling pen is an indispensable item when the work requires lines of varying widths. This instrument is designed to make sharp, neat lines which reproduce well. The standard models are used to rule straight lines. Specially constructed ruling pens mounted on a beam or compass are used to draw circles of any size.

X-acto knife

Completed paste-ups should always be neat and free from dirt specks. Rubber cement tends to ball-up on the work and may be easily removed with another ball of rubber cement. This clean-up ball may be obtained from the accumulation of cement found around the lid of the bottle. A commercial rubber cement pick-up will also remove balled-up cement without accumulating dirt as readily.

Other imperfections which cannot be removed this way may be painted over with Snopake, Hoff's White or a similar touch-up preparation. These do not flake off of the artwork and are super-white in color. Two or three thin coats are more effective than a single thick coat. Opaque white poster paint may be used to cover imperfections. However, poster paint tends to flake off and is not as white as commercial retouching media. Finished artwork should be studied for imperfections and corrected before being sent to the lithographer.

All elements of the paste-up should be pasted upon white illustration board. The surface is durable and coated so that it will accept ink without allowing it to run. Overlay copy may be pasted on clear or frosted acetate sheeting and secured at the top of the paste-up by masking tape. However, if India ink is used directly upon the overlay, frosted acetate is preferred. Clear acetate does not accept India ink as well, but because of its transparency is sometimes preferred by lithographers. Vellum tracing paper may be pasted on those areas of acetate which are to be inked or drawn upon. This will provide a good surface upon which to draw. All overlays must be in register[7] with the base color. Register marks (shown in the margin here) should be applied in diagonal corners of the paste-up before any artwork is prepared. A register mark should be placed at each corner of a larger paste-up and its overlays.

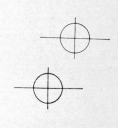

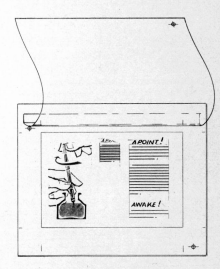

Overlay and copy

Basic Paste-Up Techniques

The paste-up artist should have an understanding of basic techniques which will produce the desired results with the greatest ease and least chance of error. Procedures which will be helpful in meeting these ends are explored here.

Major Guidelines

The first step in any paste-up is to draw accurate and properly laid out guidelines with light blue pencil. These light blue lines will drop out when photographed. The major guidelines used in paste-up work are discussed below.

Trim Size. This is the area marked to show the final size of the job after it is trimmed. Small black India ink lines at right angles in the corners

---

7. *Register.* When two or more colors are used in a piece of printing, each color must be printed from a separate plate. The proper alignment or positioning of each color is called register.

of the paste-up are usually used, in addition to the blue lines, to indicate the finished trim size.

Printed Page Size. Guidelines should be drawn on the paste-up which accurately outline the size of the printed page. Outlining helps everyone involved in evaluating the spatial relationships of the job. It also guides the pressman in positioning the image properly on the sheet. These lines must show the relation between page size and image size exactly.

Page size should not be confused with sheet size. The larger offset presses, of course, print several pages on each sheet that is run through the press.

Image Lines. This is a set of guidelines, usually drawn within the page size area, that indicates the maximum size of the image. They are drawn outside the paper area if the image is to extend to the edge of the trimmed paper. This is called a "bleed." Image lines help to align material along margins by indicating margins clearly. They also help the pressman find a satisfactory space for the "grippers" that pull the paper through the press.

Beginning a Paste-Up

Students often experience difficulty at first in spacing material properly. Problems arise in fitting the material within a particular space. There is a tendency to over- or underestimate the available space. Experience, of course, will eliminate most of these spacing problems. Experience, however, will not eliminate the need for careful planning in pre-paste-up stages. Pasted material cannot be easily moved, and careful pre-paste-up planning is a definite requirement. Listed below are eight points which will help the student to develop good spacing and make neat paste-ups.

1. Obtain all of the needed proofs, artwork and illustrations and have them at hand.

2. Draw all necessary guidelines.

3. Mount color overlays and apply register marks.

4. Trim all proofs. Remove the surplus paper margins. Be careful never to trim closer than $\frac{1}{16}''$ to the image on the proof. The $\frac{1}{16}''$ margin is used for taping on overlays. This prevents building up too many layers of superfluous material in the image area. Proofs should also be trimmed with rounded, rather than square corners. This eliminates the chance of portions folding over and covering parts of the copy.

5. Try the proofs for size. Place all of the material for a particular page or area down on the layout, but do not paste anything. Judge and study the space available. If two or more pages are to be done, facing pages should be considered as a design unit. Shift elements to get the best visual spacing. After the optimum spacing has been found, mark the position of key items in light blue pencil.

6. Begin pasting down elements. Start at the top of the layout, and work down, seeing that major elements are in the right position. This insures that everything will fit.

7. Carefully clean and touch-up the paste-up using a ball of rubber cement and a white retouching medium.

8. Cover the finished art with a suitable protective sheet. This sheet will also provide a place on which to write job specifications and related information.

In all paste-up work, the two most important factors are accuracy and cleanliness. All copy pasted down must be parallel and in the proper position. Cleanliness in the beginning stages of the offset printing process reduces stripping and opaquing time later on in the film stages.

Occasionally artwork may be added after the paste-up stage. Cross rule forms may serve as an example. Rules may be done on the paste-up, but they also may be scribed on the negatives. Scribing the negative, however, is not recommended. Some brands of film do not scribe well. Further, if the negative is lost, the artwork must be redone. If the rules are made at the paste-up stage, then additional negatives made from the paste-up will contain all of the original artwork.

Copy Reproduction

Reprinting Existing Copy. The paste-up method of copy preparation utilizes readily available art, proofs and illustrations. Since almost anything which meets the color requirements discussed above may be photographed for offset lithography, a large quantity of material becomes available to the paste-up artist. Some consideration must be given, however, to printed quality. Copyright restrictions must also be considered before including such material.

Material may be printed, reprinted and again reprinted. Each time copy is photographed, a slight loss of fidelity is introduced. The loss is usually small, and hardly detectable, yet always present. If copy is duplicated twice, the loss is twice as great. This loss increases with each reproduction until it becomes easily detectable. Letters become blurred, filled-in or broken. Make it a rule when reprinting copy to get the original piece of artwork, or the earliest printed piece available that embodies the latest corrections.

Reproducing Proofs of Type. Obtain reproduction proofs if possible. If these are not available, printed copies may be used. These should be clear and sharp. Gravure prints are usually not satisfactory, while letterpress or offset prints usually are. These prints (printed copies) must be in black or red ink on white paper to get the best results. Colored paper may sometimes be used, if the color can be removed by filtering. Light blue filters more easily than pink or red. Line art presents the same problems and offers the same advantages as duplicating text matter. Few problems will be encountered if the drawings selected are sharply rendered in black ink on white paper.

Reproducing Photographs. To preserve their tonal characteristics, continuous tone photographs are best reproduced by the halftone method. Photographic prints with extreme sharpness and maximum contrast produce the best copies. In the halftone method, the original print is photographed through a screen. The screen breaks up the various shades and tones of gray into discrete areas of black and white. The background areas and the dots create an illusion of the original values of gray when printed.

In the event an original glossy print is not available, a printed copy may be used instead. However, the new halftone will not possess the detail or range of tone values present in the original. Undesirable contrast may also have been introduced. To reduce this effect a screened, printed halftone may be reproduced by shooting it again through a halftone screen. But this yields a compromise in quality, and a moiré or "watered silk" pattern may be produced. This interference pattern may be subdued by changing the screen angle, moving the copy slightly out of focus, or making an extreme reduction.

Effects of Enlargements and Reductions. Enlarging copy tends to magnify the imperfections which are present in it. Conversely, reduction will tend to sharpen details, and minimize imperfections.

It is easier and faster to complete a paste-up somewhat larger than the finished size on some jobs. The percentage of reduction should then be indicated on the artwork. Never do a paste-up smaller than the finished size, except for large subjects such as billboards and posters.

After enlargement or reduction, the new size may be calculated by means of the slide rule, proportion scale (illustrated on cover), diagonal or mathematical ratio methods. A familiarity with these methods is required when working with enlargements and reductions.

Copyright Restrictions. While much copyrighted printed matter may be available for paste-up work, it may not be used without the permission of the copyright owner. A few words or a short phrase may be borrowed, however.

Proofs

There are seven major kinds of proofs used in the printing industry. The care used in making each kind is determined by the purpose of the proof. It is most important that the purpose be understood before pulling the proof. The tolerances, materials, care and equipment required will vary with each kind. Listed below are the common proofs in order of decreasing tolerances and increasing quality.

Galley Proofs. Proofs made from type and slugs before they are spaced out into pages or forms are called galley proofs. These proofs are used to check typographic accuracy, spelling, and conformity to original copy. Galley proofs are usually pulled on newsprint (an inexpensive pulp paper used by most newspapers). The quality standard is minimal, since the reader is interested primarily in typographic considerations. Non-drying ink is used and little care is given to image placement or margins.

Job Proofs. A proof of type and slug composition spaced out according to the layout of the job is called a job proof or page proof. The forms have been carefully spaced to exact size (or sizes) required—margins are usually indicated. These proofs show spacing and margin relationships and provide an additional check against typographical errors. Standards are somewhat higher on job proofs than on galley proofs—but, except for spacing and margins, they are still minimal. Newsprint and non-drying ink are used and are sufficient. Job proofs are frequently used to show the letterpress customer the appearance of the job before it is printed.

Revise Proofs. These are the second or third set of proofs pulled after the job or galley proofs have been corrected. Revise proofs serve as a check on the compositor. These proofs are used to make certain that all corrections and author's alterations have been made.

Reproduction Proofs. These are most carefully made, using special presses, inks, and papers. Reproduction proofs are used as original copy in paste-up work. They require close tolerances of ink, impressions, and color. The following points are considered in making reproduction proofs.

1. Inks. The inks should dry completely, without blurring or smudging. They must produce a dense black image without filling counters (enclosed areas) of type or halftone engravings.

2. Papers. These are especially designed to receive reproduction proof inks. The surface of these papers is coated so that they will record fine

details and delicate shadings. Dull and glossy finishes are available in different weights.

3. Presses. Proof presses are manufactured in a large range of sizes and features engineered for the exacting requirements of reproduction proofing. Care has been given in their construction to insure even impressions. The inking systems used lay down a uniform layer of ink. Paper guides may also be employed to keep sheets in register for color proofing.

4. Bearers. These are heavy, type-high bars positioned around the form before proofing. These bars take up roller bounce and distribute the impression evenly. They prevent smearing when the sheet is pulled away from the form, and they should be used around any form where reproduction quality is desired. The heavy rules around the outside of the form on reproduction proofs are caused by the bearers.

5. Quantity. A minimum of three reproduction proofs should be made from any form being proved. The extra proofs are invaluable to the paste-up artist for later changes, alterations or repositioning. An additional proof is usually pulled on tissue paper to provide a translucent overlay to check register.

6. Quality. Proofs used for photographic reproduction should be well inked, pulled with a firm, but even impression. Care should be exercised in recording all details such as fine lines, openings in reverses and delicate serifs. Study the proof to see that all "e", "o" and other letters with counters are not filled in. Type should be thoroughly cleaned before and after proofing. Since hand-set type tends to wear if it is used for production runs, it is best to keep a separate font and restrict its use to reproduction proofs.

Print Proofs. These are photographic prints made from lithographic negatives on light-sensitive paper. They are not made from type forms. After negatives have been made and stripped, contact prints are made in a vacuum frame on the sensitized paper which records the image on the negatives. Sometimes blue line or brown line paper is used which gives a blue or brown colored proof. If a silver halide paper is used the proof is called a silverprint. These proofs are used to determine whether all negatives have been stripped in and positioned properly. Typographical errors may still be detected at this point, but correction is more difficult and very expensive. The paste-up must be revised, new negatives shot and new film proofs made. Different negatives (e.g. color separated) may be exposed on the same sheet of sensitized paper; each will record in a different shade. Thus, two or more colors may be proved on the same sheet.

Color Key Proofs. These proofs are similar to print proofs, except that they are made on a transparent acetate with each color on a separate sheet. They are made by contacting lithographic negatives to specially treated transparent film. Their purpose is to prove negatives for work of several colors to show approximately what the finished job will look like. Each color is proved on a different sheet of acetate, corresponding to the color of the ink to be used on the press. They are then assembled as a complete color proof.

Press Proofs. A proof made by placing a job on a printing press and using the ink and paper planned for the job is called a press proof. The press, paper and ink chosen for the job are used to make the proof so that it will look exactly like the finished job. These are called for where it is important to show exact color, shade or texture before the job is run.

These proofs are given to the pressman after being checked. They are then used as the color and quality standard for the main press run. Obviously, these proofs require the usual press make-ready and color wash-ups, and thus are expensive to make.

How To Use Adhesive Lettering

Adhesive lettering has become a widely used means of preparing composition for reproduction. It is easy to use, low in cost, and can equal the best hot metal composition if care is used and some basic procedures are followed. Here are some suggestions to help the student use adhesive lettering properly. See Chapter no. 1/Study Chart (next page).

Character Alignment. Letters should always be transferred to a blue guide line to assure proper alignment. Paper with a light blue grid pattern is ideal. Check the finished line with a T square. Pre-cut or pre-aligned letters may be the best solution if you have continual difficulties with alignment.

Letter Spacing. A typographer varies his spacing to achieve maximum visual effects. This is called "spacing for color." Words ending with and beginning with "tight" letters such as l and t, need extra space. "Open" letters, such as o, a, A, and T, need less space. Similarly, adhesive letters should be studied carefully and spaced to adjust tight and open places in the line.

Die-cut letters or adhesive letters with vertical-spacing lines present an easy answer to this problem. The correct spacing between words set in capitals should be one-half em (about half the square of the type size), and one-third em (about one-third the square of the type size) for words set in lower case. Condensed and expanded faces will have to be adjusted accordingly.

Line Justification. A frequently encountered problem is that of using available line space uniformly. The key to successful justification is to plan ahead. The novice will usually start a line with liberal spacing. When he reaches mid-point, he realizes that he will not be able to complete the line in the allotted width. He begins to crowd letters to make them fit. The spacing at the beginning of the line bears little resemblance to the spacing at the end.

Mark off the middle of the line and see that the central letter of the line is placed on it. Character counts and blue-pencil guide lines can be used to budget the space more efficiently.

If a line is to be centered, set it on a sheet of paper, transferring the finished line to the artwork. It is easier to center a line after it is set than letter by letter.

Proper Adhesion. Letters must be burnished down to prevent their peeling away from the artwork during subsequent handling. Place a sheet of paper over the freshly transferred letters and burnish them down with a blunt tool. Use fresh materials and keep the artwork free of moisture and excess rubber cement.

Spelling. It is easy to misspell a word when cutting out letters and transferring them directly to the artwork. Don't spell and cut at the same time. This causes errors in spelling. Cut out or remove the letters for the line, transferring them to the edge of a ruler as you work. Then check the spelling carefully.

Finally, transfer each letter from the ruler to the artwork, using the tip of an x-acto knife blade. This extra step will actually speed up work, prevent errors, and improve spacing.

Cleanliness. Marks, smudges and fingerprints on artwork will cause inferior

QUALITY   ALIGNMENT

Use a blue guideline and a T square to correct poor horizontal character alignment.

SPACE WORDS AND LETTERS CAREFULLY

Poor letterspacing. Use one-half em space between words set in caps and one-third em space between words in caps and lower case.

DO N'T SPACE LIBERALLY AT BEGINNING

Poor budgeting of space. Spacing is liberal at the beginning of the line, too tight at the end.

get resu

Poor adhesion. Letters must be burnished down or they will peel away from the artwork.

 clear, concise

Smudges and fingerprints can be covered with white opaque.

LIGHT BLUE DROPS   PENCIL DOES NOT

Use blue pencil for guidelines. Blue drops out; dark blue or black lead pencil will not.

negatives that will require extra opaquing. Wash hands frequently. Keep tools, table top and T square clean.

A ball of rubber cement or a commercial rubber cement pick-up can be used to remove small bits of dried cement from the artwork and from around the edges of the lettering. Paint over specks and marks with white opaque. Be sure to remove all control and guide lines, except those in light-blue pencil, before the paste-up is photographed.

Types of Adhesive Lettering

Dry Transfer Letters (only the image transfers). One type of adhesive lettering is non-waxed dry-transfer lettering. The letter to be transferred is placed over the artwork and burnished directly on it. No letters need to be cut out because they are not printed on acetate. Its advantages are speed and ease of use.

However, letters are more difficult to align and letterspace since they are not on discrete pieces of acetate. The entire sheet of lettering must be handled carefully to prevent inadvertent transfer of letters.

Wax-backed Acetate Lettering. The popular material comes in a variety of faces and types, including tint screens. The alignment of letters is simplified because vertical and horizontal spacing control lines are often provided. These must be removed before the paste-up is finished. Single letters may be substituted easily by merely peeling off the old ones.

However, only a few characters are on a single sheet in the larger sizes and they can be used only once. This can be expensive. Letters must be burnished carefully or they will not adhere permanently. The wax residue near letters can be troublesome when ruling with India ink. Nonetheless, this form of lettering is most practical for general display applications on most paste-up work.

Pre-cut, Wax-backed Acetate Lettering. Pre-cutting simplifies spacing since each letter is neatly centered on its own piece of acetate. As with any adhesive, the letters are not easily transferred. This makes justification of lines more difficult.

Pre-cut, One-time Lettering Tabs. This form of display lettering is the easiest way to achieve satisfactory spacing, alignment and justification. Letters are purchased, printed on cardboard tabs, without adhesive. Letters are torn from the pad and composed in a stick similar to a type stick. Letters can be moved and spacing adjusted until justified.

Horizontal alignment is automatic. When the line is finished, a strip of tape over the line holds the letters in place. Its weakness is that the letters are not on a transparent carrier. Layers of paper can build up on artwork, and letters cannot be overlaid on drawings or other characters.

Pre-cut, Wax-backed Reusable Lettering. Single letters are printed on small pieces of wax-backed cardboard. They are widely used where large display letters are needed or where large numbers are used repeatedly.

The letters are stored in cases similar to type cases. For use, the letters are pressed onto the artwork. After the paste-up is photographed, letters are removed and saved for reuse. Since the letters are on opaque cardboard, they cannot be overlaid on other letters or drawings.

Supplementary Readings for Chapter 1

Below is a list of readings that the student and teacher may find of interest. The readings in this list are general ones, intended for use with Chapter 1 of *Modern Graphic Arts Paste-Up* Additional and briefer lists of supplementary readings are provided with each project. By making good use of these supplementary readings, the student will gain a broad understanding of the Graphic Arts.

Arnold: *Ink on Paper*, Chapter 10 (Letterpress), Chapter 14 (Lithography)

Ballinger: *Layout*, (Tools of Layout Art)

Carlsen: *Graphic Arts*, Chapter 12 (Photography)

Cogoli: *Photo-Offset Fundamentals*, Chapter 1 (Introduction to Photo-Offset Printing), Chapter 4 (Job Planning and Layout), Chapter 5 (Methods of Type Composition for Reproduction), Chapter 7 (Preparing Camera Copy for Reproduction), Chapter 21 (Legal Restrictions on Copying) and Appendix 1 (The Use and Care of Drawing Instruments)

Eastman Kodak Co.: *Basic Photography for the Graphic Arts*

Karch: *Graphic Arts Procedures—Basic*, Chapter 1 (How to Understand Printing Processes)

Karch and Buber: *Graphic Arts Procedures—The Offset Processes*

U.S. Government Printing Office: *Theory and Practice of Lithography*, Chapter 1 (Offset Copy Preparation and Phototypesetting)

Words To Know

Paste-up

Camera-ready copy

Copy

Stripping

Halftone

Window

Flat

Opaque

Vacuum frame

Dampening roller

Blanket

Ruling

Overlay

Adhesive lettering

Letter spacing

Acetate sheeting

Frosted acetate

Register marks

White opaque

Scribing

Copy preparation

Filter

Monochromatic films

Panchromatic films

Orthochromatic films

Reproduction proof

Continuous tone

Moire'

Galley proof

Press proof

Bearer

Vacuum frame

Principles of
Layout and Design

Fundamentals of a Layout

Few builders would attempt the construction of a modern multi-story office building without carefully drawn plans, drawings and blueprints. They know that these are essential to mold steel, concrete and glass into the structure they have visualized. In the same way, the printing designer uses a layout to weld paper, ink and plates into a fine piece of printing.

The layout has numerous advantages: It assures that the finished job will look as anticipated, it serves as an effective means of communication between the printer, client and advertising agency. It often uncovers efficiencies and economies, not otherwise apparent. And effective layouts are valuable sales tools. They stimulate the client's interest, making it easier to close a sale.

Another function of layouts, conveys job specifications to production people. And finally, in offset printing, the paste-up man must have a clear guide before going ahead on copy preparation. If he jumps ahead without it, he cannot lead out, or space in elements. Pasted-down copy is hard to re-position.

How to do a Layout. The most effective layouts are executed using a 4B charcoal pencil. This is a very special tool. Its effect cannot be duplicated with ordinary graphite lead pencils. Charcoal pencils can apply a wide range of tone to a sheet of paper. They can lay down dense solids, or light tones of gray. They more truly duplicate the printed image. Ordinary graphite pencils, no matter what lead, tend to lay a monotone of gray. The skilled layout artist will have two or three charcoal pencils of different hardness.

Some designers prefer to use felt tip pens to do their layouts. Some felt tip pens are available in a variety of shades. These can be used to create tone ranges similar to charcoal pencil.

The choice of paper is also important. The surface should receive charcoal pencil well. Soft book stocks such as text and antique papers are excellent. Some designers, however, prefer to use tracing paper. It is thin, has a hard surface and is translucent. They can insert various colors of paper behind the layout and simulate the finished printing job. Tracing paper is also non-porous and accepts India ink and felt tip pen well.

A good exercise to learn shading techniques is to run bands of gray from light values to dense blacks. Try making gradations which are continuous and subtle, similar to those found in the printed halftone.

Basic Layout Symbols. The object of the layout is to reflect the visual appearance of a printing job, not the written text. To help represent words, type and display copy, and illustrations, a few basic symbols, shown in Chapter no. 2/Study Chart (next page).

SMALL TYPE
(bold and light)

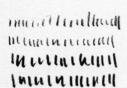

MEDIUM TYPE
(light and bold)

DISPLAY TYPE

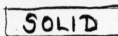

SOLID

REVERSE

TINT

PHOTOGRAPH

LINE DRAWING

Small type such as 6, 8 or 10 point is usually represented by a series of parallel lines. The weight (determined by how hard you press on the charcoal pencil), will suggest whether it is light, medium or bold face. Changing the distance between lines can suggest spacing variations. Medium size type, 12 to 18 point, may be represented by a series of wavy lines. Note the effect in Chapter no. 2/Study Chart. Larger sizes, 24 point or bigger, should be "roughed in." Sketch the feel of the letter, and the approximate weight. The same copy and wording as in the actual text helps the eye identify the display line.

Solids and Reverses. Solids and reverses may be represented by either of two techniques. You may just outline the area in pencil and write "solid" in the center. Or better yet, use the charcoal pencil to lay down an actual solid. Tint screen and shaded areas may be easily suggested by using a light pressure on the pencil, or rubbing the area with a paper rubbing stump or similar object.

Photographs may be handled in two ways. The quickest method is simply to outline the area to be occupied by the halftone. Then draw a criss-cross in the center of the box. It is better to "rough in" the major elements in the photograph in pencil. If it is a photograph, show the outline of the face and the direction it is facing. If it is an object, draw the rough outline and shade it in. Line drawings may be easily duplicated by using a sharp pencil point and making a crisp, black line.

Colored effects may also be suggested on the layout. For ordinary black and white work, use the 4B charcoal pencil or felt tip pen. But for a good color representation, use a set of pastel chalks. These are similar in nature and working characteristics to the charcoal pencil, and they come in a variety of colors.

All of the charcoal pencils and chalks discussed so far (except for felt tip pen) have one disadvantage, which is easily remedied. Lines made by these soft substances smear easily. Fixative aerosol spray should be applied on all layouts, especially those to be handled a great deal.

Three Types of Layouts

It is obvious that one can spend a great deal of time either perfecting the smallest detail in a layout, or prepare a quick representation of the finished job. The major factor which determines the care and quality of a given layout is its function. Most fall into three different types, each serving a specific use. They are the thumbnail (or miniature), the rough, and the comprehensive layouts. The following table is a summary of these layouts.

			MAJOR LAYOUTS		
TYPE	FUNCTION	SIZE	CARE IN PREPARATION	COLORS	DEGREE OF REALISM
Thumbnail	Explore ideas Develop ideas	Reduced size	Not critical	Any available	Suggestive
Rough	Visualize space and type relationships	Same size	Reasonable	Close as convenient	Approximate
Comprehensive	Show finished printed piece	Same size	Expert, great detail	Exact paper and ink	Duplicate finished job

The Thumbnail Layout. The thumbnail layout is most effective when it is done rapidly and with consideration to overall design features. It is primarily used to explore a great number of ideas.

Since the purpose is to explore, these layouts may be done small in size. About 2″ × 3″ to represent an 8½″ × 11″ page is adequate. Very little care should be given to detail, and the color of the pencil and paper used is not important.

The Rough Layout. After you have decided upon the best thumbnail, it is time to execute another layout in a little more detail. The rough layout is most useful here. It should be drawn to the same size as the finished job. Thus it will show space relationships and approximate type sizes. Reasonable care should be exercised in making this layout. Display copy should be "roughed in," and illustrations suggested in their finished position and relationship.

Enough detail should be put into this layout so that a compositor or paste-up man could put the job together. He should be able to scale halftones and read off dimensions. Color of ink and paper for the job will be specified elsewhere, rather than be reflected in the layout.

It is up to the designer to visualize what the job will look like in the chosen color and paper.

The Comprehensive Layout. The object of this layout is to leave absolutely no doubt what the finished job will look like. For the client with little imagination, or great concern about the look of the finished job, this type of layout is essential. This layout is the closest thing to the real job that the artist can put together. At first glance, it should strongly resemble the finished product, to the point of requiring a second, closer look.

To achieve this effect, the layout designer must take great care in preparation. He will use chalks, inks and paper which closely match the final job. Display lettering may be an actual type proof, or a carefully traced copy from a type book. Obviously these are expensive layouts to make and are justified only when the expense of the copy preparation and plates is high. Otherwise it would be easier to set up the type and pull a press proof and then make changes.

How To Use Color

Color perception is one of the most powerful and dynamic of the human senses. Industry has long recognized its value in interior design, packaging and marketing. For the printer and designer, color is a powerful tool. It can add a dimension and potency far beyond the limitations of the printed word or photograph.

The Dual Nature of Color. Color can react upon the mind in two distinctly different ways: (a) it can arouse an emotional response, or (b) it helps us identify the physical nature of something. An understanding of these two principles can help the printer choose the "right" color of paper and ink to suit his objectives.

Let's consider the emotional aspect of color first. All colors of the visual spectrum are placed around a circle, called a color wheel. The colors, red through yellow, are warm colors. They arouse an active, stimulating visual experience in the viewer. The colors ranging between green and violet are cold colors. They evoke a relaxing, static, cold feeling.

Psychologically it is logical to use the warm colors for subjects which are warm in nature. A color folder on the Hawaiian Islands might be most effective in reds, yellows, and oranges, while a brochure for an air conditioner can be effectively done in blues, violets and greens.

All colors develop subtle emotional responses. Bright red, sky blue, dark green, etc., all have meanings of their own. The feeling of autumn, with its changing array of hues can be created with soft browns, sepias and burnt orange. The emotional response one gets from ice, snow, wind, etc., can be generated with cold blues, violets and mauve.

A second response which color evokes is that of identification. This is based largely upon our personal experiences. We have come to know that red means danger, green means go ahead, etc. And experience has taught us that materials and objects have colors peculiar unto themselves. We associate certain colors with water, others with fire, wood, steel, hair, eyes, etc. We identify these substances partly because of their color.

Instinctively we compare the colors we see in a piece of printing with our own experience. Facial tones in a picture are compared with our real life experience with facial tones. The color of metal objects in a print are compared with real metal objects.

Color choice of printing paper and ink must depict real life as closely as possible. If your printing job shows a bunch of bananas, the color range must approximate those colors found in real life. If they do not, the viewer is immediately aware of the shortcomings. A halftone of bananas run on pink stock does not agree with our experience with bananas. Canary yellow would be a much better choice.

It is not always easy for the printer to depict true-to-life colors. Many metallic and opalescent shades cannot be reproduced in four-color process printing. Extra runs with special colors can sometimes resolve this dilemma.

People have been conditioned to accept certain combinations of colors. These seem right, pleasing and compatible . . . they are harmonious. Harmony is any system of color which creates a pleasing visual effect. There are some basic principles which have been derived from universal usage and widespread public acceptance and can be used to guide color choice.

Four color harmony patterns are widely accepted: monochromatic, analogous, complementary, and triadic. To help the printer and designer use them correctly, reference to a color wheel is advised.

1. Monochromatic color harmony is achieved when colors selected are of the same hue (color) but of varying shades and tints. Green may be chosen, for instance, and a series of related shades and tints developed by mixing in white or black ink. The product or series of shades are harmonious, since they are all related. Some pleasing multi-color effects can be achieved by choosing a given color paper and then mixing two or three shades of ink around it. The choice of paper is often the limiting factor, but fortunately inks can be mixed to develop a harmonious color scheme.

2. Analogous colors are those which are adjacent on the color wheel. For instance, red and yellow may be selected, and a series of analogous red-yellows and oranges mixed. The resultant colors are harmonious because they are related to the same two primary colors. This harmony differs from monochromatic in that two colors are used instead of one.

3. Use of complementary colors is another harmony theory. Complementary colors are the ones located on opposite sides of the color wheel. Used in proper proportions, they can produce a harmonious color effect. The major

color used should be on the cold side, and the accent color from the warm side of the wheel. For example, choose a paper color from the cold side and an ink from the warm.

4. Triadic color harmony is the fourth theory. Any three colors which form the points of an equilateral triangle will create a harmonious relationship. Of course the amounts of each color used must be considered carefully. The color of stock may be chosen as the starting point on the triangle. The major ink color as the second point and the accent color, for display lines, from the third point.

Even if all colors are carefully selected for harmony and psychological impact, problems in their use can still arise. Colors look different under various lighting conditions and surroundings.

The phenomenon known as color is due to the light-reflecting and light-absorbing quality of papers and inks. The quality of light under which the job is viewed can markedly change its appearance. For instance, under incandescent lighting, our eyes become less sensitive to red and more to blue, while under a bluish north sky light, we become more sensitive to red and less to blue. This factor can play havoc with printing jobs.

Metameric color matches are problems faced by printers and designers. In this situation two colors make a perfect match under one type of light, but look quite different under another. Many printers have had the experience of carefully matching colors in the pressroom, and after comparing the finished job in the sunlight, finding that it did not look like the color sample at all.

A designer, working under incandescent lights may choose a good color combination. The pressman, also working under the same type of light, may faithfully reproduce the designer's colors. The colors on the finished job may appear entirely different when viewed in bright sunlight.

While it would be best to choose colors and run a job in the same lighting conditions as the finished job will ultimately be viewed, it isn't always practical. An alternative is to standardize the lighting throughout all stages of production. The least variable light to view and judge color is from a moderately overcast north sky. This light is closest to neutral and presents the fewest problems. Bright sunlight, fluorescent lights and incandescent lamps all show colors differently. Printers, designers and customers should use the same standardized light source for color comparisons.

How To Select Paper and Ink

Closely related to the use of color in a printing job is the selection of paper and ink. These elements are important factors affecting the psychological impact of a finished printing job, as well as its practicality.

In the hands of the creative designer and printer, paper and ink are used to stimulate the eye, excite the emotions, shout with urgency or entice an uninterested reader. To be the master of these potent substances, the designer must understand their mechanical and esthetic qualities. The mechanical property has to to do with physical characteristics, as permanence, cost and printability. The esthetic aspects involve appearance, color and texture.

Mechanical Considerations. The initial selection of a paper or ink may be predicated on its practical use. The limitations of the printing plant or process and the ultimate environment it will be subjected to, often dictate the kind of stock or ink that must be used. Exposure to sunlight, handling, folding, cost proximity to edibles, all may affect the ground rules for selection. In addition, ability to print on special materials and plastics, availability of embossing, die-cutting and silk screening are secondary factors concerning the selection.

Printing process, stock and ink are related, and must be selected in light of each other. This implies a close coordination between designer and producer of printing.

Some practical considerations and production limitations which bear upon the primary selection of materials are:

1. Jobs with few illustrations and mostly type composition may be enriched by antique and similar coarse surface papers. These stocks impart a softness and warmth to the printed word. Obviously fine screen halftones cannot be printed letterpress on these stocks.

2. Jobs with many illustrations and halftones are ideally suited for coated and glossy finish papers. The added brilliance and sparkle given halftones justify its use, even though it does little for the text. Dull coated stocks take halftones well, and still preserve some of the mellow effects on the text. Where maximum halftone quality is desired, ultragloss coated stock is best.

3. Weight and bulk must be carefully judged if the printed piece is to be mailed or conveniently carried about. Bible papers and lightweight stocks best meet the criterion for minimum weight, postage and bulk.

4. Where folding, handling, exposure to sunlight or permanent storage is anticipated, stock and ink should be selected for their permanence and durability. A 100 percent rag bond is a better choice for a permanent document than a sulphite bond. Long-fiber boards, tag and heavy cover stocks are designed to withstand handling and folding.

5. Printability is a major consideration in the selection of printing materials. Some low grade sheets do not run well offset because of harsh chemicals and pH imbalances in them. Others do not feed well, making good register hard to obtain. Consultation with paper merchants and printing production people before making final decisions may avoid many difficulties.

6. Available basic sizes affect the selection of paper. Designers can create a variety of unique and different pieces, interesting folds and novel proportioned layouts, within these existing sizes. But troubles can result where basic sizes are not considered. A difference of $\frac{1}{8}''$ can lead to a great waste.

7. The cost of paper should be related to the function of the job. A one-time box office ticket may be successfully printed on a low grade bristol, and an annual report on a fancy cover stock, with equal success. But both may fail if the selection is reversed.

8. Finally, but not last in importance, is the fitness of stock and ink to the editorial message. Appropriate papers and layouts should be selected on their ability to communicate the message best.

Esthetic Considerations. Esthetics are interrelated with the mechanical properties of printing materials. Esthetic selection is more subtle and sophisticated than obvious mechanical considerations, such as weight or folding ability.

Two papers may weigh and cost the same, and print equally well. Yet their effect on the human mind may differ. The texture, color and thickness make the observer react in unique ways. These reactions are highly personal experiences. The successful designer understands these and manipulates them to create an effective piece of printing. An understanding of color dynamics, psychology and emotional response can give the designer valuable insights to the proper selection of printing materials.

Textured and deckle edge papers convey elegance and quality. These papers can be employed to create a mood of richness, beauty and formality. Ice blue colors may be used to suggest the cold outdoors, or warm bronzes and tans, to set a mood of softness and nostalgia.

The elements involved in the selection of paper and ink are interrelated and interactive. Samples of various inks and papers can be of great help in evaluating the total response. Many successful designers do their layouts on the stock to be used for the job and in the colors selected for the run.

Part of a successful designer's ability, is willingness to go beyond the limits of accepted patterns. He is always reaching for the new, the different, the stimulating. He will employ active elements such as die-cut pages, fold-over flips and fold-out pieces to involve the reader.

He designs alternate pages in different colors to gain variety and interest. He varies type sizes, style and uses reverses and tint screens. He uses duplex stocks and blind embossing.

The designer may use a tone-line, line resolution, tone separation, mezzo-print or wavy line tone to add vitality to the page.

The successful designer considers the entire package as an entity. The cover color may be used again as an ink color on inside pages. The envelope or outer wrap of the printed piece may be related by color, design, or stock to the whole package.

All the aesthetic and mechanical elements involved in printing design should be fused together to produce a finished piece of printing, attractive to the eye. The successful design must satisfy the customer's cost requirements and be psychologically effective. In short, it must communicate. Text, pictures, color and other graphic elements must be skillfully employed by the designer to maximize the effectiveness of the printed piece.

Supplementary Readings for Chapter 2

Arnold: *Ink on Paper,* Chapter 7 (Use of Type), Chapter 15 (Paper) and Chapter 19 (Layout)
Ballinger: *Layout,* pp. 1-96
Carlsen: *Graphic Arts,* Chapter 4 (Layout)
Cleeton, Pitkin and Cornwell: *General Printing Units* 81-89
Cogoli: *Photo Offset Fundamentals,* Chapter 4 (Job Planning and Layout)
Karch: *Graphic Arts Procedures—Basic,* Chapter 3 (How to Make Layouts) and Chapter 12 (How to Understand Paper)
Polk: *The Practice of Printing,* Chapter 22 (Layouts and Specifications)

Words to Know

Thumbnail layout	Analogous colors
Rough layout	Triadic colors
Comprehensive layout	Complementary colors
Display type	Warm colors
Solid	Cold colors
Reverse	Charcoal pencil
Tint	Line drawing
Monochromatic colors	Pastel chalk

Making a Simple Paste-Up

Introduction

The purpose of this lesson is to learn how to use basic paste-up tools, and to develop elementary paste-up skills. This lesson also develops the student's ability to evaluate space.

After completing this project, the student should be able to choose the correct size and style of typeface for a standard business card, letterhead and envelope combination.

Normally, the letterhead, envelope and business card use progressively smaller type sizes. The letterhead uses the largest type, the matching envelope is smaller and the business card uses an even smaller type size. However, there is a tendency today to use the same size type on both the envelope and the business card.

Words To Know

Harmony
Paste-up
Image area
Reproduction proof
Rough layout
Align

Materials Required

1. Basic paste-up tools

Procedure and Details

1. Obtain a piece of illustration board $11'' \times 14''$.
2. Outline the paper areas in blue pencil, in the positions shown on the rough layout. These areas should be the following sizes:
   Business card $2'' \times 3\frac{1}{2}''$
   Letterhead $8\frac{1}{2}'' \times 11''$
   Large envelope $4\frac{1}{8}'' \times 9\frac{1}{2}''$.
3. Within the above areas, outline an image area which will allow for a sufficient margin around all copy.
4. Remove the reproduction proof for this project from the book. Trim the proof carefully to within $\frac{1}{16}''$ of the image.
5. Select a harmonious grouping of type sizes from among those included.
6. Paste-up all type as shown on the rough layout. It is essential that the finished paste-up be carefully done, all lines of type pasted down parallel, and aligned in a satisfactory manner.

Supplementary Readings

Polk: *The Practice of Printing*, Chapter 33 (The Composition of Business Stationery)
Turnbull: *The Graphics of Communication*, Chapter 9 (Elements of Good Typography)
Arnold: *Ink on Paper*, Chapter 19 (Layout)
Karch: *Graphic Arts Procedures—Basic*, Chap. 3 (How to Make Layouts)

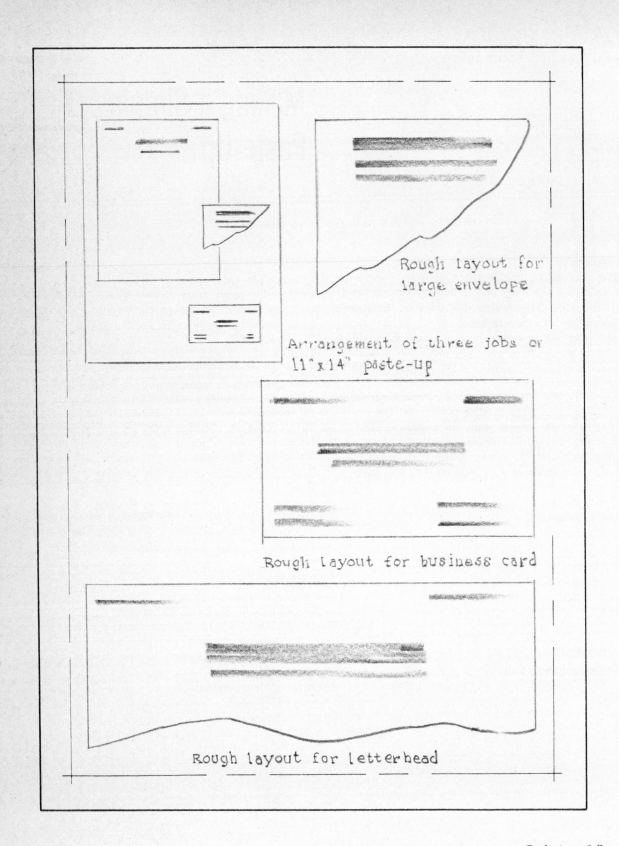

Rough layout for large envelope

Arrangement of three jobs or 11"x14" paste-up

Rough layout for business card

Rough layout for letterhead

STEVENS PRINTING CO.

STEVENS PRINTING CO.

STEVENS PRINTING CO.

STEVENS PRINTING CO.

STEVENS PRINTING CO.

STEVENS PRINTING CO.

Offset
Letterpress
Telephone
123-4567

12345 MAIN STREET
LOS ANGELES, CALIF. 90029

Offset
Letterpress
Telephone
123-4567

12345 MAIN STREET
LOS ANGELES, CALIF. 90029

Offset
Letterpress
Telephone
123-4567

12345 MAIN STREET
LOS ANGELES, CALIF. 90029

12345 Main Street	*12345 Main Street*	**12345 Main Street**
Los Angeles, Calif. 90029	*Los Angeles, Calif. 90029*	**Los Angeles, Calif. 90029**
Offset	*Offset*	**Offset**
Letterpress	*Letterpress*	**Letterpress**
James Stevens	*James Stevens*	**James Stevens**
Sales Dept.	*Sales Dept.*	**Sales Dept.**
12345 Main Street	*12345 Main Street*	**12345 Main Street**
Los Angeles, Calif. 90029	*Los Angeles, Calif. 90029*	**Los Angeles, Calif. 90029**

Project no. 1/Proof

Color Considerations

Introduction

Many colors are available for a printing job. However, the paste-up artist is limited in choosing colors to be used on the paste-up itself, since all elements will be copied photographically.

When orthochromatic film is used, all elements to be photographed on the paste-up should be in black or dark red ink. All elements that are not to be photographed may be done in light blue. The intensity of the color, as well as its hue, is important in determining whether or not it will photograph with the films used in lithography.

In addition to color, the artist must understand the effects of photographing continuous tone copy (photographs) when using high contrast orthochromatic film. This lesson illustrates the effect of photographing these various media with orthochromatic film.

Words To Know

Orthochromatic
Intensity
Continuous tone copy
Opaque
Contrast
Screened photographs

Materials Required

1. Basic paste-up tools
2. A continuous tone photograph and other pieces of artwork
3. A means of making and developing an orthochromatic negative
4. A typewriter

Procedure and Details

1. Outline an $8\frac{1}{2}'' \times 11''$ paper area, and then a $7\frac{1}{2}'' \times 10''$ image area within the paper area on a piece of illustration board.
2. Type the descriptions indicated on the rough layout. Paste these down on the board.
3. Obtain a continuous tone photograph, and paste it down as indicated on the rough layout.
4. Obtain the other artwork required, and paste each down above its proper identification. Include a sample of pen, pencil and crayon as indicated on the rough layout.
5. Cover the finished paste-up with a protective cover.
6. Shoot a line negative of the paste-up, using high contrast orthochromatic film.
7. Develop the negative. Do not opaque or retouch it in any way.
8. Compare the negative with the paste-up.
9. Make a list of those colors which did not pick up on the film.
10. Describe the effects upon the film of reproducing the continuous tone photograph. Did it increase or decrease in contrast? Did the negative preserve all of the delicate values of gray?

Supplementary Readings

Cogoli: *Photo-offset Fundamentals,* Chapter 7 (Preparing Camera Copy for Reproduction)

Eastman Kodak: *Basic Photography for the Graphic Arts,* p. 1-45

Karch: *Graphic Arts Procedures—Basic,* Chap. 8 (How to Understand Letterpress Printing Plates)

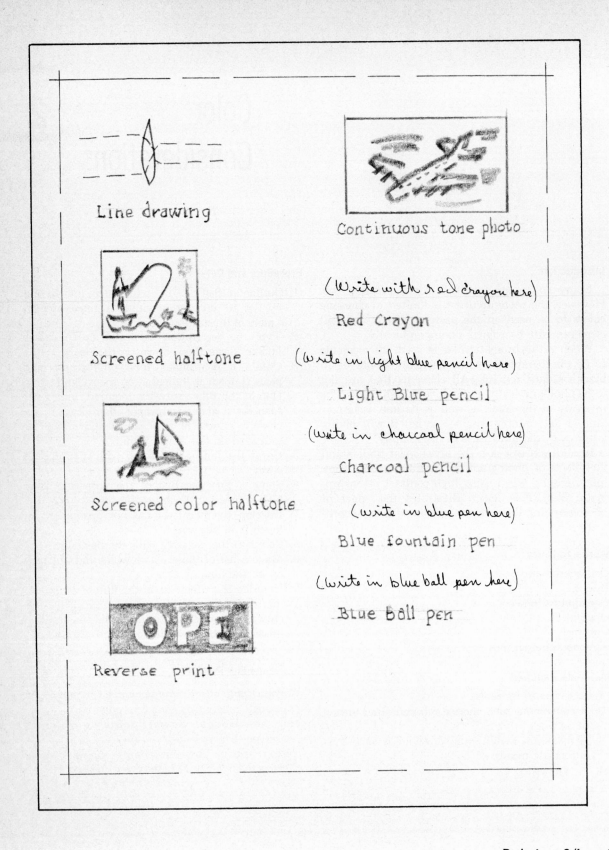

Line drawing

Continuous tone photo

Screened halftone

(Write with red crayon here)
Red crayon

(Write in light blue pencil here)
Light Blue pencil

(Write in charcoal pencil here)
Charcoal pencil

Screened color halftone

(Write in blue pen here)
Blue fountain pen

(Write in blue ball pen here)
Blue Ball pen

OPE

Reverse print

Proofreaders' Marks

Introduction

Understanding proofreaders' marks and using them correctly are important tasks for anyone involved in paste-up, copy preparation and printing. (See next page.) The paste-up artist must be acquainted with the various marks so that he may read the marks made on paste-ups that are to be corrected.

In letterpress printing, corrections are usually marked directly on galley proofs. Final job proofs may then be pulled to see that all changes have been properly made.

In offset printing there are some differences in procedure. Type may be set and galley proofs pulled as in the letterpress method. Revised proofs may be called for in some cases. Then, reproduction proofs are made. These are finished quality proofs that are to be photographed. They are used directly on the paste-ups. If an error is detected after they are pasted down, special care must be exercised in marking and making corrections. Since these are to be photographed, any marks made should be such that they will not photograph. This lesson suggests a method of indicating errors in finished artwork and proofs which will not interfere with later photographic reproduction.

Words To Know

Copy preparation
Galley proof
Job proof
Reproduction proof

Materials Required

1. Basic paste-up tools
2. Translucent tracing paper

Procedure and Details

1. Outline a paper area of 6″ × 9″ and then an image area of 3½″ × 7½″ within the paper area on a piece of illustration board.
2. Paste down the reproduction proof entitled "Offset" in the center of the image area.
3. Cover the paste-up with a sheet of tracing paper, secured at the top with masking tape.
4. Mark all of the typographical errors described below. Be sure to follow these rules:
   a. Always mark the errors on the tracing paper, never on the proof itself.
   b. Proofreaders' marks consist of two parts: a mark in the body indicating the location of the error, and a mark in the margin, indicating the nature of the error. Be sure to connect both marks with a line.
   c. Use only standard proofreaders' marks.
   d. If marks *must* be made on the proof itself, be sure to use light blue pencil, and note the change on the tracing paper overlay.

Errors to be Marked on the Tracing Paper:

1. Indicate the broken letter "S" in the display line.
2. Change the comma in the fifth line of the first paragraph to a period.
3. Change the capital "P" in the fifth line of the first paragraph to a lower case "p."
4. Indicate a wrong font (typeface) "T" in the second line of the second paragraph.
5. The word "type" is misspelled, in the fifth line of the second paragraph.
6. There is a broken letter in the sixth line of the third paragraph.

Supplementary Readings

Arnold: *Ink on Paper*, Chapter 9 (Proofreading)
Karch: *Graphic Arts Procedures—Basic,* Chap. 6 (How to Prepare Manuscript and Proofread)

standard proofreaders' marks

Delete; to take out	No indention	Insert query
To insert	Move to right	Insert exclamation point
Insert matter omitted	Move to left	Insert hyphen
Take out and close up	Move up	Insert one em dash
Let it stand	Move down	Insert acute accent
Wrong font	Align (horizontally)	Insert grave accent
Lower case letter	Align (vertically)	Insert umlaut or diaeresis
Set in upper and lower case	Transpose (word or letter)	Insert circumflex or "doghouse"
Set in caps	Center (word or line)	Insert cedilla
Set in small caps	Close-up	Insert tilde
Set in caps and small caps	Broken letter	Insert parentheses
Set in roman	Equalize space	Insert brackets
Set in italics	Letterspace	Insert ellipsis
Set in italic caps	Take out letterspace	Insert asterisk
Set in boldface italics	Insert space	Insert dagger
Superior figure	Insert period	Insert double dagger
Inferior figure	Insert comma	Invert or turn around
Begin a new paragraph	Insert semicolon	Push down space
No paragraph; run in	Insert colon	Spell out
Indent one em	Insert apostrophe	Query to author
Indent two ems	Insert quotes	Break for new line

EXAMPLE

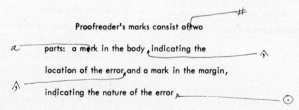

Proofreader's marks consist of two parts: a mark in the body, indicating the location of the error, and a mark in the margin, indicating the nature of the error.

OFFSET

All of the elements that are to be printed in this job are first set in type. The lines are proof-read and any corrections are then made in the lines. The type is then removed from the stick and placed on a galley. A Proof of the type is made, This proof, together with other elements which are necessary, are gathered and pasted down on a sheet of paper.

The paste-up is then photographed in a process camera, and a negative is made. This negative is stripped, and a lithographic plate is made. The lithographic plate is then mounted on a lithographic press, and copies are printed. The typ is placed back in the type case seeing that all spacing material is also returned to its proper place in the shop.

After the type is set, a galley proof is made on newsprint. Any corrections in the type are marked on the newsprint galley proof. After these corrections are made, another galley proof on newsprint is made. If the copy is set correctly, a reproduction proof is made. Care must be taken to see that all letters on the "repro" are proofed sharply, and that there are no broken letters.

A good grade of smooth white paper is used to make the reproduction proofs. Best results are obtained when the student obtains heavy rules or borders, and places them around the form being proofed.

These "bearers" prevent letters on the end of the line from smearing during the proofing operation. A photograph made from a reproduction proof cannot be any better than the proof. It is essential that the proof be sharp, properly inked and spaced properly.

The Point System

Introduction

Knowledge of the printers' point system is important in understanding and handling paste-ups. This system is the accepted standard of communicating dimensions in the printing industry. It should be learned as one of the preliminary steps to any work in the Graphic Arts. This project will familiarize the student with the point system, and enable him to understand it.

The printers' point system consists of the following measurements:

1 point* = 1/72 inch
1 nonpareil = 1/12 inch or 6 points
1 pica = 1/6 inch or 12 points
6 picas = 1 inch or 72 points

Newspaper advertisements are measured in *agate* lines which are 5½ points high.

Words To Know

Point

Nonpareil

Pica

Agate line

Line gauge

Print trimmer

Lead

Slug

Materials Required

1. Basic paste-up tools
2. Printer's line gauge or pica rule
3. Photographic print trimmer or other means of accurately cutting rectangles of paper to precise sizes
4. Black paper

Procedure and Details

1. Outline a paper area 9″ × 12″, and an image area 8½″ × 11″ on a piece of illustration board.
2. Using the line gauge, trim seven squares of paper to the exact dimensions specified in the rough layout.
3. Paste these down in the positions shown, and cover the completed paste-up with a protective cover.

Supplementary Readings

Polk: *The Practice of Printing*, Chapter 10 (The Printer's Point System)

Arnold: *Ink on Paper*, Chap. 4 (Printer's Terms)

Turnbull: *The Graphics of Communication*, Chap. 4 (Type and Type Faces)

Karch: *Graphic Arts Procedures—Basic*, Chap. 4 (How to Set "Hot" Type)

---

*Note: One point is actually .0138 inch for foundry type and .014 inch for Intertype and Linotype. For practical purposes, however, the measurements given above are used.

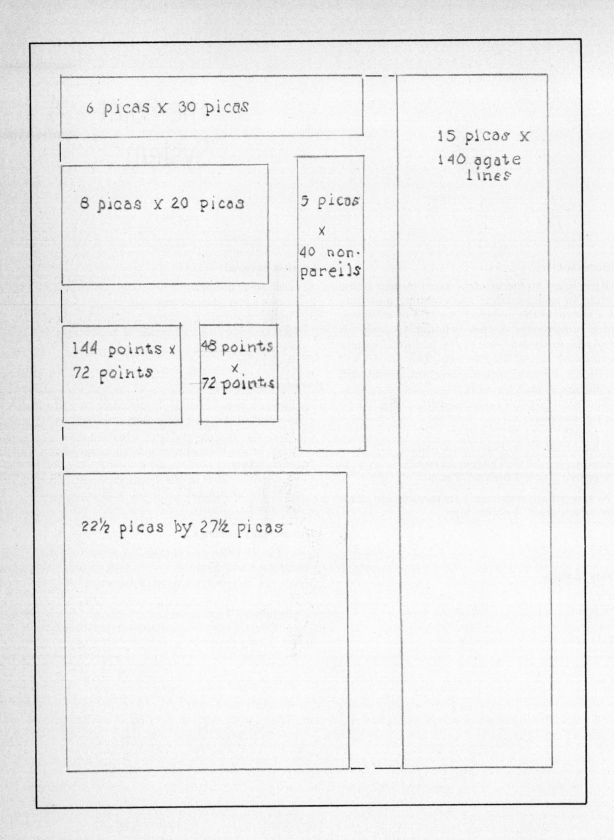

6 picas x 30 picas

15 picas x
140 agate
lines

8 picas x 20 picas

5 picas
x
40 non-
pareils

144 points x
72 points

48 points
x
72 points

22½ picas by 27½ picas

Project no. 4/Layout

Legibility of Typefaces

Introduction

This project results in a paste-up of type specimens, grouped together for comparison of legibility. Many factors affect the legibility of a typeface. Among these factors are: size, style, and weight of the typeface chosen. The white space around the text, spacing between lines and width of lines should also be considered. The type and finish of the paper and the color of ink used also contribute to or detract from the readability of the printed page. This lesson will explore one of the factors, that of type style.

Words To Know

Legibility
Weight
Style
Type size

Materials Required

1. Basic paste-up tools.
2. Adhesive lettering.

Procedure and Details

1. Outline a paper area of 9″ × 12″ and an image area of 8″ × 10″ on a piece of illustration board.

2. Using adhesive or wax-backed lettering, set the display line "Legibility" and paste it down as shown (see rough layout).
3. Remove the facsimile reproduction proof from this book and paste the blocks of copy down as shown on the rough layout.
4. Stand the paste-up on a table at a distance of 3 feet from the eye.
5. Rank all eight specimens in order of legibility, with the most legible, first.
6. Compare your ranking order with other members of the class. Do they all agree? What can you conclude from this subjective comparison?
7. Cover the finished paste-up with a protective cover.

Supplementary Readings

Cleeton and Pitkin: *General Printing*, Unit 88 (How to Choose a Type Face)
Polk: *The Practice of Printing:* Chap. 24 (Legibility in Printed Matter)
Turnbull: *The Graphics of Communication:* Chap. 9 (Elements of Good Typography)
Karch: *Graphic Arts Procedures—Basic*, Chap. 3 (How to Make Layouts) and Chap. 2 (How to Know the Various Type Faces)

Legibility

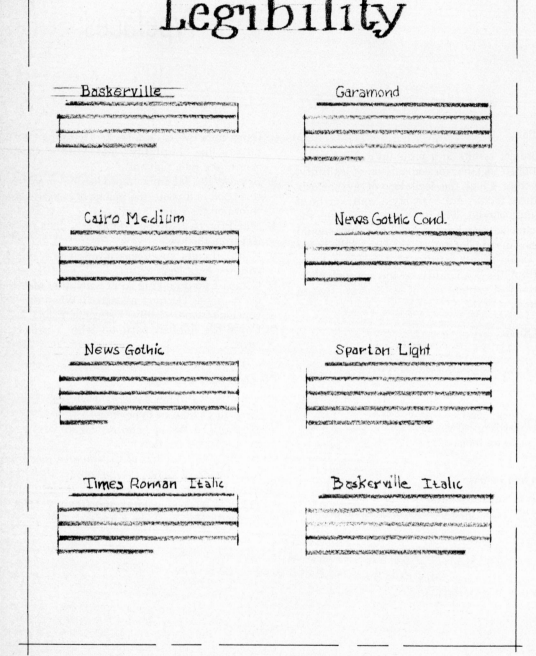

Baskerville

Garamond

Cairo Medium

News Gothic Cond.

News Gothic

Spartan Light

Times Roman Italic

Baskerville Italic

Project no. 5/Layout

A basic function of printing is to communicate ideas. Legible typefaces make it easier for the reader to grasp the ideas presented in the text.

A basic function of printing is to communicate ideas. Legible typefaces make it easier for the reader to grasp the ideas presented in the text.

A basic function of printing is to communicate ideas. Legible typefaces make it easier for the reader to grasp the ideas presented in the text.

A basic function of printing is to communicate ideas. Legible typefaces make it easier for the reader to grasp the ideas presented in the text.

A basic function of printing is to communicate ideas. Legible typefaces make it easier for the reader to grasp the ideas presented in the text.

A basic function of printing is to communicate ideas. Legible typefaces make it easier for the reader to grasp the ideas presented in the text.

A basic function of printing is to communicate ideas. Legible typefaces make it easier for the reader to grasp the ideas presented in the text.

A basic function of printing is to communicate ideas. Legible typefaces make it easier for the reader to grasp the ideas presented in the text.

Common Type Sizes

Introduction

It is particularly helpful for the offset or letter-press craftsman to be able to identify and visualize common type sizes. The paste-up man should also become familiar with those that are in wide use today. This lesson will expose the student to these sizes, and will also help him develop hand letter-ing and ruling skills.

Words To Know

Nonpareil
Pica type
Agate line
Brevier
Long Primer
Line gauge

Materials Required

1. Basic paste-up tools
2. Type specimens, ranging from 6 through 48 point, 30 picas wide
3. Black India ink
4. Speedball pens and holder
5. Ruling pen

Procedure and Details

1. Outline a paper area of 8½″ × 11″ and an image area of 7½″ × 10″ on a piece of illustra-tion board.
2. Hand letter (with Speedball pen) the words "Common Type Sizes", in black India ink, as shown in the rough layout.
3. Draw two 6-point rules, 8″ long as shown (use the ruling pen).
4. Obtain and paste down specimens of 6, 8, 10, 12, 14, 18, 24, 30, 36 and 48 point type as indicated on the rough layout. These may be obtained from magazines, newspapers, brochures or any other clearly printed source.
5. Label each specimen using a small tip Speed-ball pen.
6. Be sure to consider carefully the available mar-gins and white space. Allow ample margin around, and space between, each specimen.
7. Cover the finished paste-up with a protective cover.

Supplementary Readings

Polk: *The Practice of Printing,* Chap. 10 (The Print-ers' System of Measurement)
Karch: *Graphic Arts Procedures—Basic,* Chap. 3 (How to Make Layouts)

Note that the letters in each point size are smaller than the size given. Point size always designates the body of the type on which the character sits. There is always some shoulder and therefore the characters measure somewhat smaller than the point size.

How is one to assess and evaluate a type face — 6 point

How is one to assess and evaluate a type — 8 point

How is one to assess and evaluate — 10 point

How is one to assess and — 12 point

Redevelopment is a word much used — 14 point

However it is neither in this — 18 point

The name of quality — 24 point

Overland Touring — 30 point

Magazine of the — 36 point

Periscoping — 48 point

Metropolis of — 60 point

Geographical — 72 point

Project no. 6/Study Chart

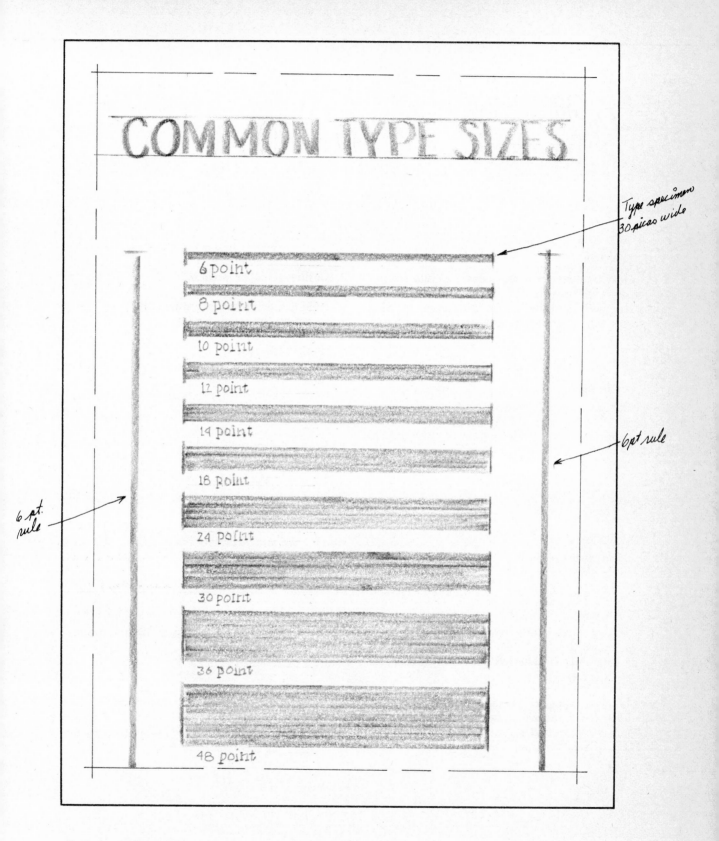

COMMON TYPE SIZES

6 point

8 point

10 point

12 point

14 point

18 point

24 point

30 point

36 point

48 point

Type specimen
30 picas wide

6 pt rule

6 pt.
rule

7 Classifying Typefaces

Introduction

Most type styles in use today fall into six major classes. These are text, script, roman, sans serif, square serif and italic. An awareness of these classes will be of help to anyone designing, specifying or planning printing jobs.

Words To Know

Text	Square serif
Script	Modern type
Roman	Oldstyle
Sans serif	Ascender
Italic	Descender

Materials Required

1. Basic paste-up tools

Procedure and Details

1. Outline a paper area of 8½″ × 11″, and an image area of 7½″ × 10″.
2. Rule a 4-point border around the paste-up, as shown on the rough layout.
3. Paste down all of the type specimens in the positions indicated.
4. Paste down the body copy on the reproduction proofs where indicated.
5. Cover the finished paste-up with a protective cover.

Supplementary Readings

Cleeton and Pitkin: *General Printing,* Unit 95 (The Genesis of Type Faces)

Polk: *The Practice of Printing,* Chap. 23 (Classification of Type Faces)

Arnold: *Ink on Paper,* Chap. 7 (Use of Type)

Karch: *Graphic Arts Procedures—Basic,* Chap. 2 (How to Know the Various Type Faces)

Text is immediately recognizable — you may have known it before under the name Old English. The name *text* is preferred as a classification, because it is a generic term.

San Serif types are unadorned, characterized by the fact that they have no serifs. (The word *sans* is French in origin and means without. A serif is a finishing stroke on a letter or character.

Square serif types are rugged in appearance. They have blunt, square serifs. They reflect a mechanical precision.

Roman faces are the most common typefaces. Almost all books are done in a roman face.

Italics are the slanted types. Almost all roman types have an accompanying italic face.

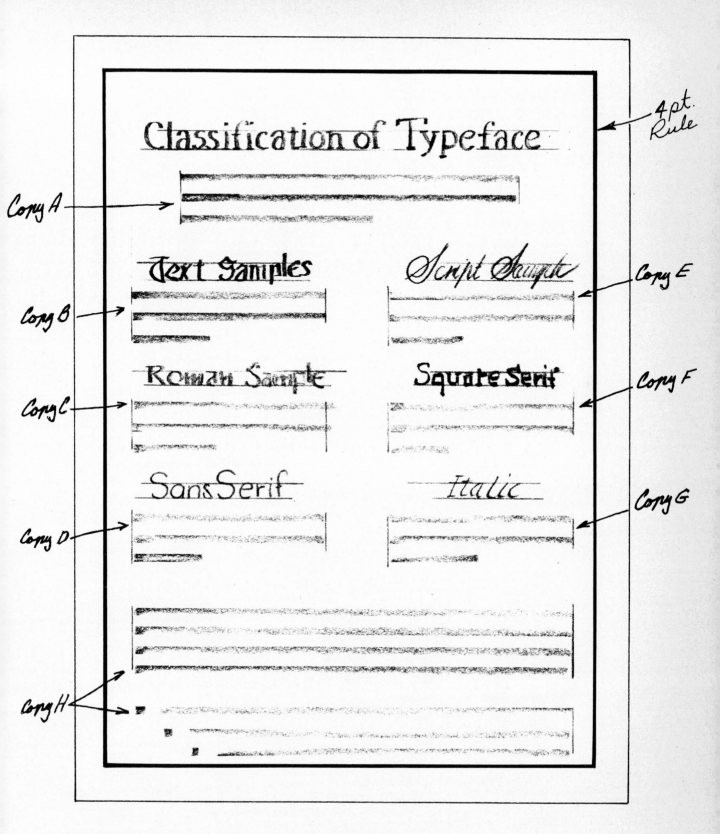

Classification of Typeface

4pt. Rule

Copy A

Text Samples   *Script Sample*   Copy E

Copy B

Roman Sample   **Square Serif**   Copy F

Copy C

Sans Serif   *Italic*   Copy G

Copy D

Copy H

Classification of Typefaces

- PROPER COMBINATION OF TYPE STYLES
  - CORRECT SPACING OF TYPE ELEMENTS
    - RELATION OF TYPE STYLE TO PRINTED MATERIAL
      - READABILITY AND LEGIBILITY

GOOD TYPOGRAPHIC DESIGN IS NOT A MATTER OF ARBITRARY CHOICE OR TYPE STYLES, BUT THE RESULTS OF A CONSIDERED EVALUATION OF MANY CONSIDERATIONS. IT IS THE EXERCISE OF GOOD JUDGMENT AND TASTE IN MATTERS AS . . .

Copy H

All of the type styles in use today, fall into one of the broad, general classifications below. It is convenient to be able to identify types in these classes so that they may be used and mixed harmoniously.

Copy A

SQUARE SERIF LETTERS: As shown above, types with serifs were patterned after early stone-cutter letters. The strokes are approximately uniform in weight, and have straight unbracketed serifs.

ITALIC LETTERS: Designed by Aldius Manutius in 1501, these letters are close fitting and slanting. They may be used to contrast with Roman type forms, though large masses set in italic are hard to read.

TEXT LETTERS: Above is an example of a text letter. Note the angular letter forms which are suggestive of the medieval scribes. These are used largely in social printing.

ROMAN TYPES: These are easily read types which are traditional in character. The letters are formed with heavy strokes and contrasting light elements. They are easily read when set in large masses.

SANS SERIF LETTERS: This is an example of a popular contemporary type style. The letters have no serifs, and reflect simplicity and strength, stripped of all unnecessary adornment.

SCRIPT LETTERS: The sample above illustrates a type group which denotes a hand lettered or written effect. This style of lettering adds contrast and color to a printed piece.

Copy F

Copy G

Copy B

Copy C

Copy D

Copy E

Italic

Roman Sample

Sans Serif

Square Serif

Script Sample

𝕿𝖊𝖝𝖙 𝕾𝖆𝖒𝖕𝖑𝖊

Making a Layout

Introduction

To obtain a pleasing appearance, each printing job should be the result of a plan. The care exercised in making the plan will vary, depending upon the time available, quality of the job, and other factors. Where possible, the student should develop the habit of making a plan or *layout* for each job.

There are three common types of layouts: the thumbnail sketch, the rough layout and the comprehensive. The *thumbnail* is a small, quick drawing. Several of these are usually done to explore different possibilities. The *rough layout* is made with more care, and is the one most frequently used. It gives a indication of the size, weight and style of type chosen. The *comprehensive layout* is a carefully drawn precise plan showing all detail. This layout is used when it is necessary to show what the final job will look like before production begins.

This project will explore the thumbnail and rough layouts. A number of designs will be considered, then a rough layout will be prepared. From the rough layout, type will be set, and a paste-up completed.

Words to Know

Thumbnail
Rough
Comprehensive

Materials Required

1. Basic paste-up tools
2. A 4B charcoal pencil or felt tip pen
3. Hand composition facilities

Procedure and Details

1. Execute a number of thumbnail layouts of Copy A.
   Use a 4B charcoal pencil or a felt tip pen to create different line weights.
   Consider a number of different design approaches to the problem, both modern and traditional.
   The finished paper size should be 6″ × 9″.
2. Pick the best thumbnail design and prepare a rough layout from it. This should be done to the finished size of the job. Indicate by varying the pencil stroke, the size, style and weight of the typefaces you choose.
3. Set type, following the rough layout. Try to match the layout in terms of spacing and general placement. Pull a newsprint proof and correct any errors.
4. Pull three reproduction proofs.
5. Paste a reproduction proof on a piece of illustration board, using the extras for possible corrections. You may discard these reproduction proofs when finished.
6. Cover the finished paste-up with a protective cover.

Supplementary Readings

Carlsen: *Graphic Arts,* Chap. 4 (Layout)
Turnbull: *The Graphics of Communication,* Chap. 10, (Principles of Layout and Design)
Ballinger: *Layout,* entire book
Polk: *The Practice of Printing,* Chap. 22 (Layout and Specifications)
Karch: *Graphic Arts Procedures—Basic,* Chap. 3 (How to Make Layouts) and Chap. 5 (How to Set Cold Type)

COPY A

    For the finest Commercial Printing
      Call:
        YOUR NAME PRINTING CO.
        Your company address
        Your city and state
        Your telephone number
Our modern facilities are at your
disposal ... may we have the opportunity of bidding on your next job?
We shall be happy to prepare a layout
and cost estimate at no charge.

    OFFSET AND LETTERPRESS PRINTING

Specialists in:
   • Business Cards
    • Envelopes
     • Letterheads
      • Commercial printing
We have a completely equipped, modern
printing plant to handle all of
your needs. All work is produced
with consideration given to:
   • Quality
    • Effectiveness
     • Sales appeal
      • Fitness of paper and type
       styles
For prompt, quality printing, call
us now!

Learning to Use White Space

Introduction

Any printed piece has two complementary design aspects: The printed areas, and the non-printed areas. They are both subject to the designer's manipulation. The non-printed areas are often referred to as white space, or negative space. It is necessary for the printing designer to be aware of the importance of white space, since it affects the readability, appearance and effectiveness of the design. This lesson presents a design problem in using white space effectively. When planning the paste-up, an effort should be made to judge spatial relationships and make optimum use of white space.

Words To Know

Negative space
White space

Materials Required

1. Basic paste-up tools
2. Large display letters (Obtain from any clearly printed source)
3. Ruling pen
4. No. 2 sable brush

Procedure and Details

1. Outline a 9″ × 12″ paper area, on a piece of illustration board.
2. Plan, and then outline a pleasing image area for the 9″ × 12″ size paper.
3. Hand letter, in black India ink, the two display words "Layout" and "Design" approximately 60 points high.
4. Using the ruling pen, rule an 18-point and a 6-point solid rule as shown.
5. Remove the facsimile reproduction proof from this book.
6. Paste down the two paragraphs of copy, as shown in the rough layout. The widths of these paragraphs bear an important relationship to the negative or white space areas.
7. Position the two large display letters. Plan the white space areas around each letter.
8. Cover the finished paste-up with a protective cover.

Supplementary Readings

Carlsen: *Graphic Arts*, Chap. 4 (Layout)
Turnbull: *The Graphics of Communication*, Chap. 10 (Principles of Layout and Design)
Ballinger: *Layout*, entire book

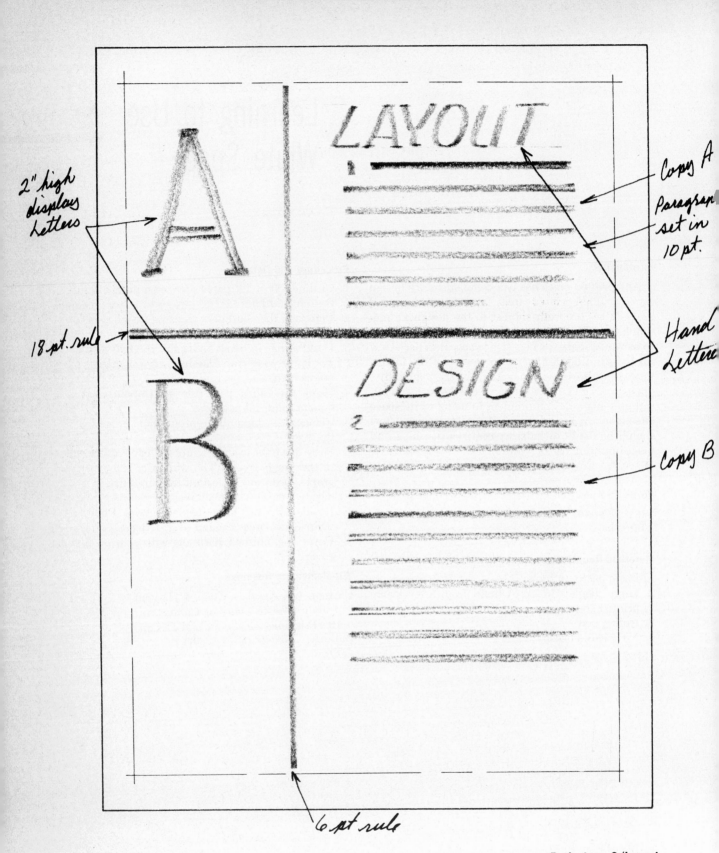

2" high display letters

18 pt. rule

Copy A

Paragraph set in 10 pt.

Hand Lettered

Copy B

6 pt. rule

COPY A

A good layout is the essential first step in planning and producing a printed piece. It serves as a guide for others working on the job, from the estimating department to the bindery department. The effort invested in the careful planning and laying out of a job will be repaid many times. It provides a place in which to explore designs before work is actually begun on the printed piece. A layout may be changed, redesigned or improved, without incurring any production expenses. Costs rise sharply when type has to be reset, or printing plates remade.

COPY B

A design should be based upon some logical principle, plan or order which lends itself to artistic appreciation. The subtleties which form the basis for much contemporary design are often unobserved by those schooled in the strict confines of traditional design philosophy. Therefore the successful design need not conform to the rigidities of formal balance. It does mean that all parts of the design be integrated, or bear a relationship to one another. Therefore, artists and designers rely upon such devices as axes, pivot points, space relationships and type harmony in order to achieve a unity of elements in the design. Without some cohesive relationship, the design will appear as a disturbing assortment of pictures, type and illustrations.

Grouping and Planning Copy

Introduction

One of the most difficult things to learn in elementary paste-up work is the proper utilization of available space. It is often difficult for the beginner to judge the amount of space needed for a given amount of copy. Overestimating and underestimating often occur, thus requiring either deletion or addition of copy, or extensive manipulation.

An effort should be made to estimate the amount of material which can be fitted into a given area. With experience, the artist will be able to adjust minor spacing as he proceeds. Try to develop a feel for this. Make an effort to group material into logical units and provide adequate space around all illustrations and blocks of copy.

Words To Know

Shape harmony
Page contour

Materials Required

1. Basic paste-up tools
2. Speedball pen and holder
3. Black India ink.
4. A halftone, line drawing and reversed block of copy (Obtain from any clearly printed source)
5. Ruling pen.

Procedure and Details

1. Outline a paper area of $8\frac{1}{2}'' \times 11''$, and an image area of $7\frac{1}{2}'' \times 10''$.
2. Using the ruling pen, rule a 6-point rule, 10 inches long as shown.
3. Carefully trim all proofs. Do not trim closer than 1/16 inch to the margin.
4. Gather together all of the proofs and artwork required in this project.
5. Place all of these elements down on the illustration board, in their approximate final position.
5. Visually evaluate the spacing, shifting elements to improve margins and grouping.
7. Begin pasting down the proofs and artwork, starting at the top. Be particularly careful to keep the elements in their allotted space.
8. Cover the finished paste-up with a protective cover.

Supplementary Readings

Ballinger: *Layout*, entire book
Turnbull: *The Graphics of Communication*, Chap. 10 (Principles of Layout and Design)
Polk: *The Practice of Printing*, Chap. 28 (The Principle of Shape Harmony)
Karch: *Graphic Arts Procedures—Basic*, Chap. 3 (How to Make Layouts)

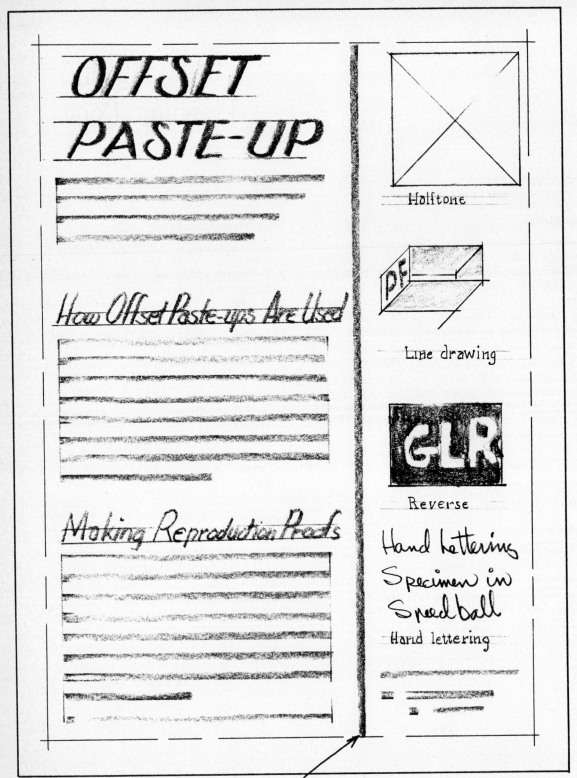

OFFSET
PASTE-UP

How Offset Paste-ups Are Used

Making Reproduction Proofs

Halftone

Line drawing

GLR

Reverse

Hand Lettering
Specimen in
Speedball

Hand lettering

6-pt. solid rule

PASTE-UP OFFSET

How Offset Paste-ups Are Used Making Reproduction Proofs

TODAY'S MODERN PRINTING TECHNIQUES
REQUIRE OFFSET AND LETTERPRESS
PROCESSES BOTH BE USED IN THE
PREPARATION OF MANY PRINTING
JOBS. THIS JOB IS SET IN TYPE
AND WILL BE PRINTED
BY OFFSET.

After the type is set, a galley proof is made on newsprint. Any corrections in the type are marked on the newsprint galley proof. After these corrections are made, another galley proof on newsprint is made. If the copy is set correctly, a reproduction proof is made. Care must be taken to see that all letters on the "repro" are proofed sharply, and that there are no broken letters.

A good grade of smooth white paper is used to make the reproduction proofs. Best results are obtained when the student obtains heavy rules or borders, and places them around the form being proofed.

These "bearers" prevent letters on the end of the line from smearing during the proofing operation. A photograph made from a reproduction proof cannot be any better than the proof. It is essential that the proof be sharp, properly inked and spaced properly.

All of the elements that are to be printed in this job are first set in type. The lines are proof-read and any corrections are then made in the lines. The type is then removed from the stick and placed on a galley. A Proof of the type is made. This proof, together with other elements which are necessary are gathered, and pasted down on a sheet of paper.

The paste-up is then photographed in a process camera, and a negative is made. This negative is stripped, and a lithographic plate is made. The lithographic plate is then mounted on a lithographic press, and copies are printed. The type is placed back in the type case, seeing that all spacing material is also returned to its proper place in the shop.

HALF-TONES   LINE DRAWING

HAND LETTERING   REVERSE

Center and Off-Center Layouts

Introduction

Printing layouts generally fall into two design categories. They are the center and the off-center, sometimes called symmetrical and asymmetrical layouts. It is important for the student to understand the distinctions between these two types. The symmetrical layout is best for jobs with a formal, traditional motif and the asymmetrical is best for modern themes. This lesson suggests a minimum of copy and details, and the student is encouraged to develop his own ideas and designs.

Words to Know

Symmetrical
Asymmetrical
Traditional
Axis
Contemporary
Optical center

Materials Required

1. Basic paste-up tools
2. A 4B charcoal pencil
3. Obtain copy, drawings and photographs from any clearly printed source.

Procedure and Details

1. Prepare two rough layouts of an advertisement, using a 4B charcoal pencil. One should be of the center and the other of the off-center type. Use your judgment on spacing and design. Be sure to include all the elements required in each paste-up.
2. Complete a paste-up, using a formal center layout. Be sure that it contains:
   a. A paper area of $8\frac{1}{2}'' \times 11''$
   b. Two halftone photographs of different sizes
   c. Three paragraphs of copy
   d. One line drawing
   e. A rule completely around the job.
3. Complete a paste-up, using an off-center layout. Be sure that it contains:
   a. A paper area of $8\frac{1}{2}'' \times 11''$
   b. One $4'' \times 6''$ halftone
   c. Three paragraphs of copy
   d. A large display line of copy
   e. One line drawing
4. Cover both paste-ups with a protective cover.

Supplementary Readings

Ballinger: *Layout*, entire book
Turnbull: *The Graphics of Communication,* Chap. 10 (Principles of Layout and Design)
Karch: *Graphic Arts Procedures—Basic,* Chap. 3 (How to Make Layouts) and Chap. 6 (How to Prepare Manuscripts and Proofread)

Points to Remember Regarding Center Layouts
1. They embody conservative type sizes and styles.
2. They are usually employed with traditional subjects.
3. They contain a single axis down the center of the sheet.
4. Any treatment to the left side of the design is followed by a similar treatment on the right side.
5. They tend to lack vitality.

Points to Remember Regarding Off-Center Layouts
1. They embody unique word and copy spacing.
2. They embody unique line and illustration spacing.
3. They usually have more than one design axis, and these may be located away from the optical center.
4. They embody extreme type styles and weights.
5. They embody extreme contrast of type sizes.
6. They are usually employed with modern, contemporary subjects.
7. They tend to be interesting and dynamic.

Simple Newspaper Paste-Up

Introduction

Many small daily and weekly newspapers are printed by the offset process. This requires pasting up copy into full pages. Photographs are handled by using black "windows" on the artwork (called windows because they produce transparent areas on the negative) and later stripping of the halftone negatives made from the photographs.

A popular way of referring to column heads is by their size. The width in columns and the number of lines used to describe the head (e.g. 2 column by 2 line).

Among the various front-page styles in use today is the balanced or formal front page make-up. This is a symmetrical layout. Exceptions may be made in order to add interest and vitality to the design. A perfectly balanced page, down to the minutest detail, lacks interest and appears dull.

Words to Know

Window
Column head
Page make-up
Galley proof
Hairline

Materials Required

1. Basic paste-up tools
2. Newspaper galley proofs of columns and heads (use an ordinary newspaper)
3. Ruling pen
4. Black India ink
5. Photographic print trimmer

Procedure and Details

1. Outline a 15″ × 21″ image area on a piece of 16″ × 24″ illustration board.
2. Rule guidelines for eight vertical columns, using light blue pencil.
3. Use black hairline rules to divide columns.
4. Paste down the proofs of columns and heads as shown in the rough layout.
5. Where an illustration is shown, paste down a square piece of black paper.
6. Cover the finished paste-up with a protective cover.

Supplementary Readings

Turnbull: *The Graphics of Communication,* Chap. 15 (Newspaper Typography and Make-up)

Karch: *Graphic Arts Procedures—Basic,* Chap. 1 (How to Understand Printing Processes); Chap. 2 (How to Know the Various Type Faces); Chap. 11 (How to Do Letterpress Work); and Chap. 12 (How to Understand Paper)

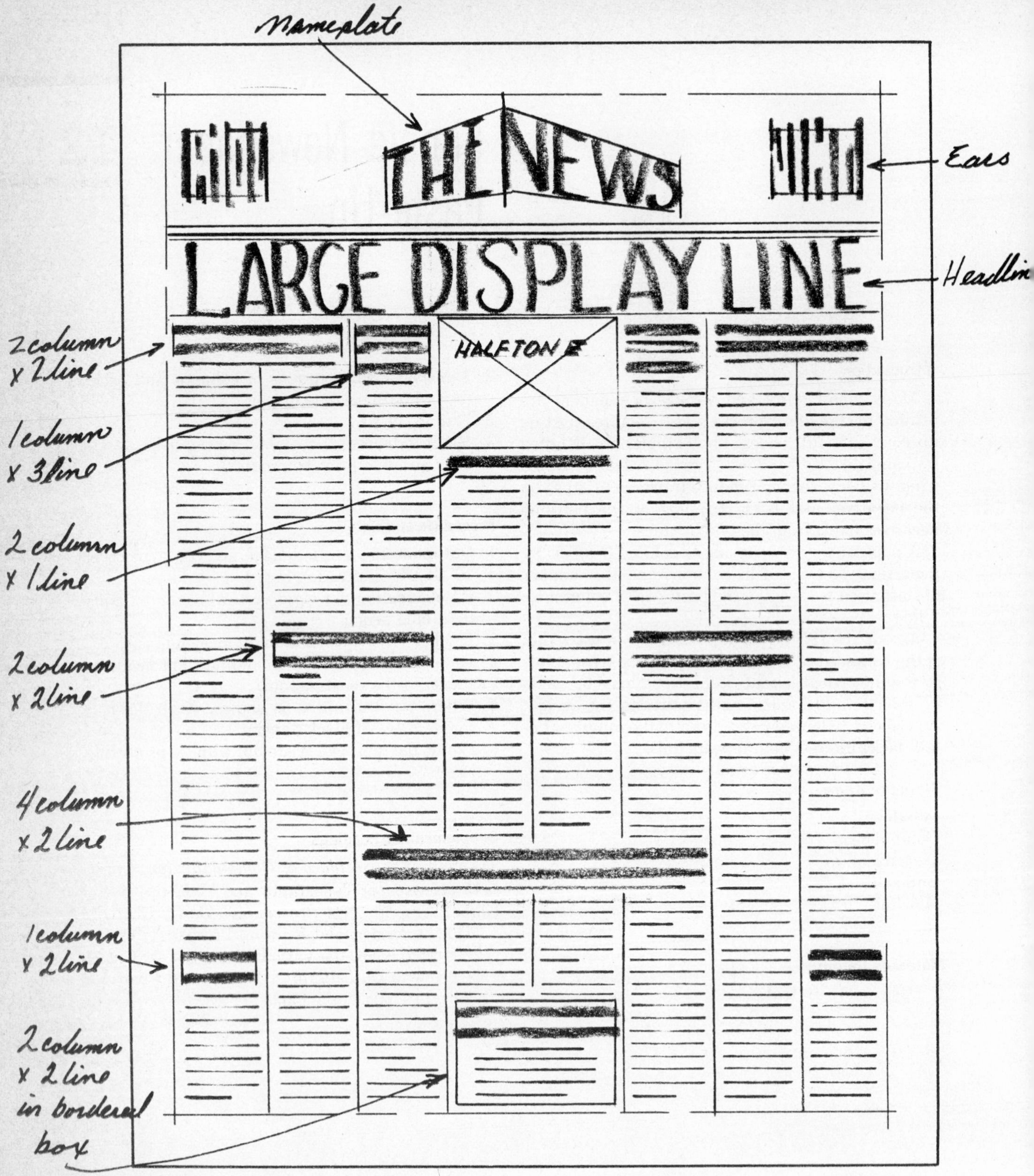

Nameplate

THE NEWS

Ears

LARGE DISPLAY LINE

Headline

2 column x 2 line

1 column x 3 line

HALFTONE

2 column x 1 line

2 column x 2 line

4 column x 2 line

1 column x 2 line

2 column x 2 line in bordered box

Project no. 12/Layout

Learning to Use Adhesive Lettering

Introduction

Adhesive lettering is available in sheets that have printed letters on one side, and a wax backing. They are used by cutting out the desired letters and pressing them into place on the artwork. They are then burnished firmly with a blunt instrument. Some adhesive lettering is manufactured with an image which will transfer directly to the paste-up by applying pressure to the face of the sheet. The most difficult phase of working with adhesive lettering is in alignment of letters, and spacing. This must be carefully done in order to yield alignment which is as accurate as that found in typeset proofs.

Words to Know

Burnish
Alignment

Materials Required

1. Basic paste-up tools
2. Sheets of adhesive lettering
3. Ruler
4. Burnishing tool
5. Sharp x-acto knife

Procedure and Details

1. Outline a paper area of 8½" × 11", and an image area of 6" × 9".

2. Set the eight lines of copy indicated on the rough layout with adhesive letters.
3. Follow this procedure when using adhesive lettering:
   a. Carefully cut around the desired letter. Be sure to include any guide and spacing lines. Do not cut entirely through backing sheet
   b. Remove each letter, and place it along the edge of a ruler. Handle the letters with the tip of the x-acto knife.
   c. Transfer letters to the ruler, rather than directly to the artwork. This will permit a double check on spelling and speed the work.
   d. Rule a horizontal blue line on the artwork to indicate the final position of the letters.
   e. Transfer each letter from the ruler to the blue line, be certain that spacing is even, and all letters are properly aligned.
   f. Trim off any excess spacing marks from below each line.
4. Cover the completed paste-up with a protective cover.

Supplementary Readings

Cogoli: *Photo-Offset Fundamentals*, Chap. 5, (Type Composition for Reproduction)
Karch: *Graphic Arts Procedures—Basic*, Chap. 5 (How to Set Cold Type)

YOUR NAME

TITLE OF CLASS

Care must be taken with adhesive
lettering to preserve alignment.

L E T T E R S P A C E   L I N E

Adhesive lettering is a
flexible medium with
which to work.

Learning to Use Rubylith® Film

Introduction

Rubylith® film is a red film which is coated over a plastic base. This film is placed over any area on the paste-up that is to be printed as a solid. It is then fastened at the edge. This produces an "overlay." This overlay may be used either as a photographic negative (and is then considered a "mechanical" overlay), or it may be photographed, and thus produce a negative. In the former method, it is used to expose the plate directly.

This material can be used as a fast means of preparing mechanical overlays for color separation. It is superior to black paper or black India ink because of its uniformity. Rubylith® film is supplied in a red color which permits it to be used directly over sensitized emulsions. Amberlith is a similar material, amber in color, which may be used over artwork. These materials eliminate hand brush work, and may be used to produce masks, drop-outs and open-window negatives.

Words to Know

Mechanical overlay
Overlay
Color separation
Mask
Drop-out
Open window negative
Register marks

Materials Required

1. Basic paste-up tools
2. Rubylith® film
3. X-acto knife
4. Ruling pen

Procedure and Details

1. Outline a paper area of 6″ × 9″, and an image area of 5½″ × 8½″. Rule the graph shown in the rough layout with India ink and a ruling pen.
2. Paste down the type supplied in the reproduction proof, referring to the rough layout for placement.
3. Obtain a piece of Rubylith® film 7″ × 10″ or larger, and mount it directly over the paper area. Secure it at the top with masking tape.
4. Using a straightedge and an x-acto knife carefully cut away all areas of the film indicated on the rough layout. Be sure that you remove only the colored film layer, and not the plastic backing also.
5. Using a marking pencil, label the overlay "Color" and the illustration board "Black."
6. Cover the entire paste-up, and overlay with a single protective cover.

Supplementary Readings

Turnbull: *The Graphics of Communication*, Chap. 14 (Color in Printing)
Arnold: *Ink on Paper*, Chap. 12 (Color Printing)
Cogoli: *Photo-Offset Fundamentals*, Chap. 10 (Color Reproduction)

Rubylith® Ulano Products Company, Inc.

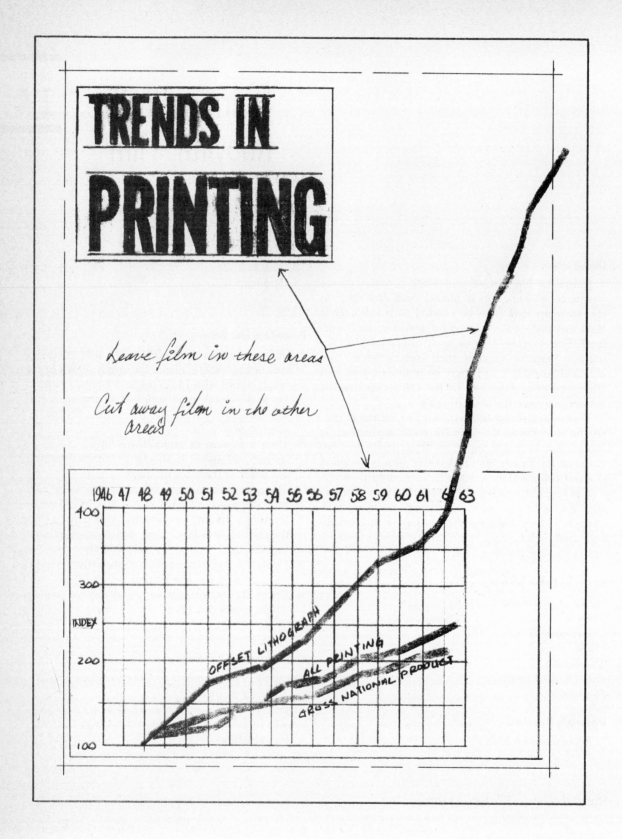

TRENDS IN PRINTING

Leave film in these areas

Cut away film in the other areas

1946 47 48 49 50 51 52 53 54 55 56 57 58 59 60 61 62 63

400

300

INDEX

200

100

OFFSET LITHOGRAPH

ALL PRINTING

GROSS NATIONAL PRODUCT

TRENDS IN
PRINTING

OFFSET LITHOGRAPHIC PRINTING		400		200	100	300
ALL PRINTING						
GROSS NATIONAL PRODUCT						
INDEX	1946	47	48	49		50
		57	58	59		60
	51	52	53	54	55	56
		61	62		63	

Making Corrections in Typewriter Composition

Introduction

There are several techniques available to the paste-up artist to help him to make simple corrections, alterations and copy changes in any of the typewriter methods of cold type composition. The correct choice of method will often save much time and effort, particularly where there are many changes. The student should familiarize himself with as many alternatives as possible in order to facilitate the work.

The three most common methods of correcting typewriter composition are listed below.

1. If a single word is misspelled, retype the word correctly on a separate sheet of paper. Then, lay the corrected word over the misspelled one, using a light table, or back-lighted glass. Carefully align the correction over the error. Cut out a box around the misspelled word, being sure to cut through both sheets of paper. Discard the misspelled word. Place a strip of tape behind the hole in the proof. Using a pair of tweezers or knife blade, place the corrected word in the position previously occupied by the error. Press the correction down firmly on the tape.

2. If a group of words, or an entire line is incorrect, retype the entire line on a separate sheet of paper. Using a T square, carefully cut out the incorrect line, and paste or tape the correctly typed line in place.

3. If an entire paragraph is typed incorrectly, or is to be changed, simply retype the paragraph, and paste it over the one that is incorrect.

Words to Know

VariTyper
Alteration

Materials Required

1. Basic paste-up tools
2. VariTyper or standard typewriter
3. Cellophane tape

Procedures and Details

1. Type the text entitled COPY A. Set the margins on the typewriter to produce a 4″ wide column. Single space the lines, and double space between paragraphs. Use ordinary white typing paper.
2. Type the text entitled COPY B. Also use a 4″ wide column and ordinary white typing paper. These will be the changes and alterations to be incorporated into COPY A.
3. Outline a paper area of 6″ × 9″, and an image area of 5½″ × 8″ on a piece of illustration board.
4. Using adhesive lettering, set the display words COLD TYPE on a piece of paper, and paste it down on the artwork.
5. Using COPY B, make all of the changes below in the text of COPY A.
   a. Correct the word "setting" in paragraph 1.
   b. Correct line 3 of paragraph 2.
   c. Correct the entire third paragraph.
6. Paste the corrected COPY A in the center of the image area.
7. Cover the paste-up with a protective cover.

Supplementary Readings

Cogoli: *Photo-Offset Fundamentals,* Chap. 5 (Type Composition for Reproduction)
Karch: *Graphic Arts Procedures—Basic,* Chap. 5 (How to Set Cold Type)

COPY A

Cold-type is a method of preparing material for offset reproduction, without actually seeting type or making plates. A typewriter is used to "set" the type, and this image is copied and printed by photo-offset methods.

Since no type is set, an error detected in the copy is not corrected by meeely changing the slug.It is necesary to make the correction by a different means than the usual hot metal methods. Some of these methods of correcting typing errors have been discussed. If you make a typing error, correct the error in one of the ways discussed in this project.

These methods, if used properly, will produce copy, in which, the extent of the corrections will be imperceptable.

COPY B

(Type this material on a 4" wide column, double space between groups.)
setting

by merely changing the slug. It is necessary to make the correction by a

These methods, if used properly, will yield copy in which the corrections will be imperceptible.

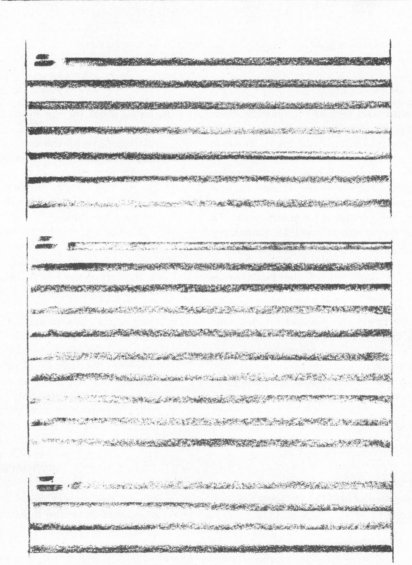

16 Revising a Paste-Up

Introduction

Changes in copy and text are frequently made before printing jobs are rerun. When making changes, the paste-up artist should use as much of the previously set material as he can, in order to keep typesetting costs low. When a large number of changes must be made however, it may be best to reset the entire job. If a particular typeface is no longer available, the paste-up artist must use what he has, as far as this is possible. Sometimes a printed piece is used for the revised paste-up. He may have to build his corrections from words or letters found in a duplicate of the piece he is correcting.

This lesson consists of taking two reproduction proofs from a previously run job and revising one, using elements from the other where necessary. This will give the student the opportunity to evaluate various methods of making copy changes and alterations. Some of the correction methods from Project 15 may be employed here.

Materials Required

1. Basic paste-up tools

Procedure and Details

1. Outline a paper area of $8\frac{1}{2}'' \times 11''$ on a piece of illustration board.
2. Make the following changes in one proof using the extra proof for the needed elements.
   a. Remove the phrase "guidance and a direct relationship with the community," from paragraph one. Place a period at the end of paragraph one.
   b. Delete the section entitled "ENROLLED." Distribute the extra space between the remaining sections.
   c. Underline the words "No tuition" in the fifth paragraph, using a ruling pen.
   d. Using a cold-type method, add a display line to the top of the form: "Midtown Technical College." Use a script style of lettering, if available.
   e. Correct the last paragraph to read "95,500 volumes and 415 periodicals." (Cut out a window, and place the new letters and numbers from the extra proof behind the window.)
   f. Correct "PURPOSE" in the first paragraph to read "PURPOSES."
   g. In the fourth paragraph, correct to read, "regular day faculty and experts from business and industry."
   h. Using a cold-type method, add "APPLICATIONS BEING ACCEPTED NOW!" as the last line of the job.
   j. Mount the revised piece on the illustration board and cover the finished paste-up with a protective cover.

FACT SHEET

PURPOSE

A two-year free public junior college. Offers many Occupational-Terminal curricula, through many departments leading to the Associate in Arts degree, vocational competence and employment; the two-year Lower Division Curricula (Transfer) prerequisite to the two-year Upper Division at a State College or University leading to a Bachelors degree; general education; guidance and a direct relationship with the community.

FOUNDED

1929. 34 acre campus; 190 classrooms; 67 buildings.

ENROLLED

Men 8906   Women 6601
Day 7214   Evening 8293
(Day load 2-18 units,   Evening load 3-9 units)
Will probably transfer before completing A.A. degree. 75 percent have had no college work; has a part-time job; drives own automobile; average age is 19 years; majors in Business, Education or Liberal Arts.

FACULTY

Selected on a District-wide basis after examination and placement on an eligibility list. Masters degree in academic fields and State Teachers Credential. Evening faculty are regular day and experts from business and industry.

COSTS

No tuition. Student Body membership $6.50 day, $2.50 evening, each semester.

SESSIONS

Two regular, one summer.
Day classes—8 a.m. to 4 p.m.
Evening classes—4 p.m. to 10 p.m.

ASSOCIATE IN ARTS DEGREE

60 total units of course credit including 20 toward a well-defined objective.
Grade point average of 2.0 (C).
Completion of 15 units in regular status during last semester, including 6 units of History and Constitution, 6 units of communication and 4 units of health and physical education.

SERVICES

Audio-Visual—provides teaching aids and equipment.
Counseling—guidance and counseling on personal and academic problems.
Health—first aid, health information and counseling, medical examinations for new students.
Library—95,000 volume and periodicals
Placement—part-time jobs for students and full-time for graduates.
Student Activities—student government, athletics, and club program financed by student membership funds.

FACT SHEET

PURPOSE

A two-year free public junior college. Offers many Occupational-Terminal curricula, through many departments leading to the Associate in Arts degree, vocational competence and employment; the two-year Lower Division Curricula (Transfer) prerequisite to the two-year Upper Division at a State College or University leading to a Bachelors degree; general education; guidance and a direct relationship with the community.

FOUNDED

1929. 34 acre campus; 190 classrooms; 67 buildings.

ENROLLED

Men 8906   Women 6601
Day 7214   Evening 8293
(Day load 2-18 units,   Evening load 3-9 units)
Will probably transfer before completing A.A. degree. 75 percent have had no college work; has a part-time job; drives own automobile; average age is 19 years; majors in Business, Education or Liberal Arts.

FACULTY

Selected on a District-wide basis after examination and placement on an eligibility list. Masters degree in academic fields and State Teachers Credential. Evening faculty are regular day and experts from business and industry.

COSTS

No tuition. Student Body membership $6.50 day, $2.50 evening, each semester.

SESSIONS

Two regular, one summer.
Day classes—8 a.m. to 4 p.m.
Evening classes—4 p.m. to 10 p.m.

ASSOCIATE IN ARTS DEGREE

60 total units of course credit including 20 toward a well-defined objective.
Grade point average of 2.0 (C).
Completion of 15 units in regular status during last semester, including 6 units of History and Constitution, 6 units of communication and 4 units of health and physical education.

SERVICES

Audio-Visual—provides teaching aids and equipment.
Counseling—guidance and counseling on personal and academic problems.
Health—first aid, health information and counseling, medical examinations for new students.
Library—95,000 volume and periodicals
Placement—part-time jobs for students and full-time for graduates.
Student Activities—student government, athletics, and club program financed by student membership funds.

Estimating
Tint Screen Values

Introduction

Tint screens are widely used throughout the Graphic Arts industry to produce shading, background and other design effects. These screens are produced in a variety of *densities* (percentage of area covered by dots), and a variety of *rulings* (number of lines of dots per inch). A screen of any given density may be obtained in a variety of rulings.

It will be helpful for the student to be able to identify these various tint screen values. In order to do this, collect some samples and study them under a pocket magnifying glass, rather than with the naked eye. This will make it easier to compare the samples with the enlargements in the Study Chart. The student will soon learn to distinguish the characteristics of each screen value.

Words to Know

Pocket magnifier
Ben Day screen
Screen value

Materials Required

1. Basic paste-up tools
2. Pocket magnifier (Linen tester)
3. Various specimens of screen values. (Obtain these from a clearly printed magazine or brochure.)

Procedure and Details

1. Study the illustrations of various screen densities. Compare the area covered by the dots to the open area.
2. Using a pocket magnifier, identify and cut out a series of 1″ × 2″ density samples ranging from 10% through 90%. Comparison will be easier if these samples are of the same ruling and in black ink.
3. Using a pocket magnifier, identify and cut out a series of 1″ × 2″ ruling samples ranging from 60 lines per inch through 150 lines per inch. Comparison will be easier if these samples are of the same density and in black ink.
4. Outline a paper area of 8½″ × 11″ on a piece of illustration board.
5. Paste the group of density samples (10% through 90%) in a single column down the left edge of the paper. Label the percentage of each.
6. Paste the group of ruling samples (60 through 150 lines) in a single column down the right edge of the paper. Label the rulings per inch of each.
7. Cover the finished paste-up with a protective cover.

Supplementary Readings

Sayre: *Photography and Platemaking for Photo-Lithography*
Turnbull: *The Graphics of Communication*, Chap. 6 (Plates for Letterpress Printing)
Arnold: *Ink on Paper*, Chap. 11 (Printing Plates)
Karch: *Graphic Arts Procedures—Basic*, Chap. 8 (How to Understand Letterpress Printing Plates)
Cogoli: *Photo-Offset Fundamentals*, Chap. 7 (Preparing Camera Copy for Reproduction)

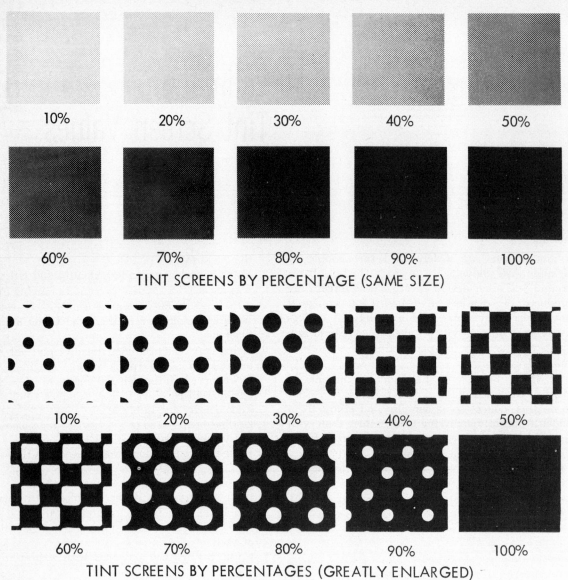

10% 20% 30% 40% 50%

60% 70% 80% 90% 100%

TINT SCREENS BY PERCENTAGE (SAME SIZE)

10% 20% 30% 40% 50%

60% 70% 80% 90% 100%

TINT SCREENS BY PERCENTAGES (GREATLY ENLARGED)

60 LINE   65 LINE   85 LINE   100 LINE   110 LINE   120 LINE   133 LINE   150 LINE

RULINGS PER INCH (SAME SIZE)

Project no. 17/Study Chart

SAMPLE OF SCREEN DENSITIES		SAMPLE OF RULINGS
	10% 60 line	
	20% 65 line	
	30% 85 line	
	40% 100 line	
	50% 110 line	
	60% 120 line	
	70% 133 line	
	80% 150 line	
	90%	

1" X 2" specimens of screen densities in this column

1" X 2" Specimens of screen in this column

Project 18 Using Tint Screens

Introduction

This lesson explores the application and handling of wax-backed tint screen materials. They may be used to produce shading, background and texture effects. Tint screens come in a wide variety of patterns as well as densities and rulings. It is important to learn how to use these interesting materials properly.

Words to Know

Burnish
Craftint
Zip-A-Tone
Contak
Texture pattern

Materials Required

1. Basic paste-up tools
2. Sharp x-acto knife
3. Sheets of wax-backed tint screen material

Procedure and Details

1. Outline a paper area of 6″ × 9″, and an image area of 5½″ × 8½″, on a piece of illustration board.
2. Using adhesive lettering, set the words "QUICK" and "TINT" on pieces of paper, and apply these to the artwork as shown in the rough layout.
3. Remove the facsimile reproduction proof from the book. Take the two paragraphs of 8 pt. type, and paste these down as shown.
4. Apply two areas of tint screen material, as shown in the rough layout. Follow these rules, when using wax-backed tint screen material:
   a. Use a sharp knife.
   b. Use a light blue pencil to outline the area to be screened.
   c. Remove a section of screen from its paper backing, and place it lightly over the area to be covered.
   d. Gently press the piece into temporary position.
   e. Carefully cut around the area to be covered, using a steel edge, and an x-acto knife.
   f. Remove the surplus material from the areas not to be screened.
   g. Burnish down the remaining sections of screen to produce a smooth, uniform wax bond.
5. Cover the finished paste-up with a protective cover.

Supplementary Readings

Turnbull: *The Graphics of Communication,* Chap. 6 (Plates for Letterpress Printing)
Arnold: *Ink on Paper,* Chap. 11 (Printing Plates)
Karch: *Graphic Arts Procedures—Basic,* Chap. 8 (How to Understand Letterpress Printing Plates)
Cogoli: *Photo-Offset Fundamentals,* Chap. 7 (Preparing Camera Copy for Reproduction)

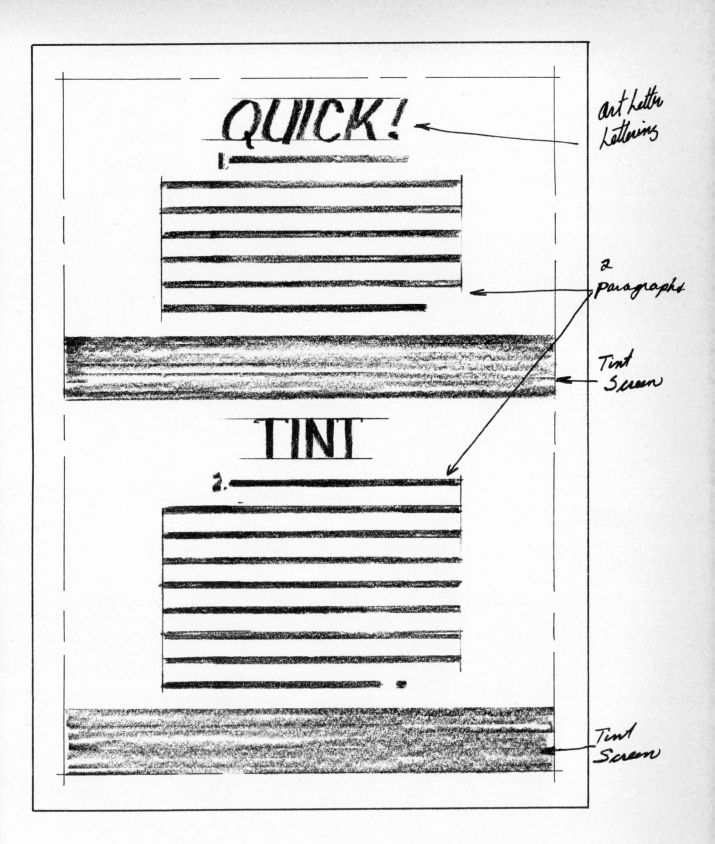

It is often desirable to add variety to a printed page by using tint screen material. This is available on wax-backed acetate sheets. The material is removed from the backing sheet, and gently placed over the artwork. Next, it is rubbed down on those areas that are to receive the screen. A sharp knife is then used to trim away any excess. This method is a fast, easy way to apply shading, texture and tint patterns.

The idea of using a screen to make tint and shading patterns was invented by an English engraver, Ben Day. Any material used to create a tint effect is today called a Ben Day tint. He experimented by inking screens, and transferring the wet ink to plates before they were engraved. Today, however, most lithographers do not use this method, but instead employ the wax-backed material. For fine screens, 100 lines per inch and over, lithographers prefer to strip-in screened negatives directly into the film. This avoids the tendency of fine screens to fill in or plug up when rephotographed.

Using
the Ruling Pen

Introduction

The ruling pen is one of the most useful and effective tools available to the paste-up artist. This instrument can be of great help in all work with solids, rules and cross-rule forms. The ruling pen is designed to produce fine, uniform ink lines ranging in size from a hairline through three points wide. Wider lines and solids may also be made by ruling in the perimeters and inking in the center with a small sable brush.

With the increased use of the photo-offset method to produce business forms, the ruling pen takes on more importance. This lesson develops the student's skills in handling, adjusting and maintaining the ruling pen.

Words to Know

Hairline	Nibs
Sable brush	Cross-rule work
Rule form	Bow compass

Materials Required

1. Basic paste-up tools
2. Ruling pen
3. Black India ink
4. No. 2 sable brush
5. Straightedge

Procedures and Details

1. Outline a paper area of $8\frac{1}{2}'' \times 11''$, and an image area of $8'' \times 10\frac{1}{2}''$, on a piece of illustration board.
2. Complete the exercise shown on the rough layout. Follow these directions when using the ruling pen:
   a. Hold the pen slightly inclined away from the wet ink.
   b. Fill the pen by placing ink only *between* the nibs. Do this by using the applicator supplied with each bottle of ink. Release a small amount of ink from the applicator directly between the nibs of the pen. Never dip the pen directly into the bottle of ink.
   c. Always work the pen against a straightedge. This will produce a uniform line.
   d. Place washers or masking tape under the straightedge to raise it slightly from the paper. This will prevent it from smearing the wet ink.
   e. Never rule lines wider than 3 points in a single pass of the pen. For rules wider than 3 points make a series of passes, moving the straightedge a little each time.
   f. For large solids, and extremely wide rules (over 18 points), rule in only the perimeter. Then fill in between these lines with a fine sable brush. These perimeter rules should be about 6 points wide to make filling in easier.
   g. Do not fill the pen with ink more than $\frac{1}{4}''$ from the tip at one time. Any excess might drop out on to the artwork.
   h. On cross-rule work, be sure to allow sufficient time for the ink to dry before ruling right angle lines.
   i. To lend a neat finished appearance to a series of parallel lines, rule the lines $\frac{1}{8}''$ beyond the margin, and trim the sheet to align the rules.
   j. When ruling corners, rule one line beyond the intersection, and come back with white opaque and "dress up" the corner.
   k. Always wash the pen in warm water, immediately after finishing.
   l. Do not allow ink to dry in the pen.
   m. Store the pen with the adjustment screw open, to relieve the pressure on the nibs.
3. Cover the finished paste-up with a protective cover.

Supplementary Reading

Cogoli: *Photo-Offset Fundamentals,* Appendix I

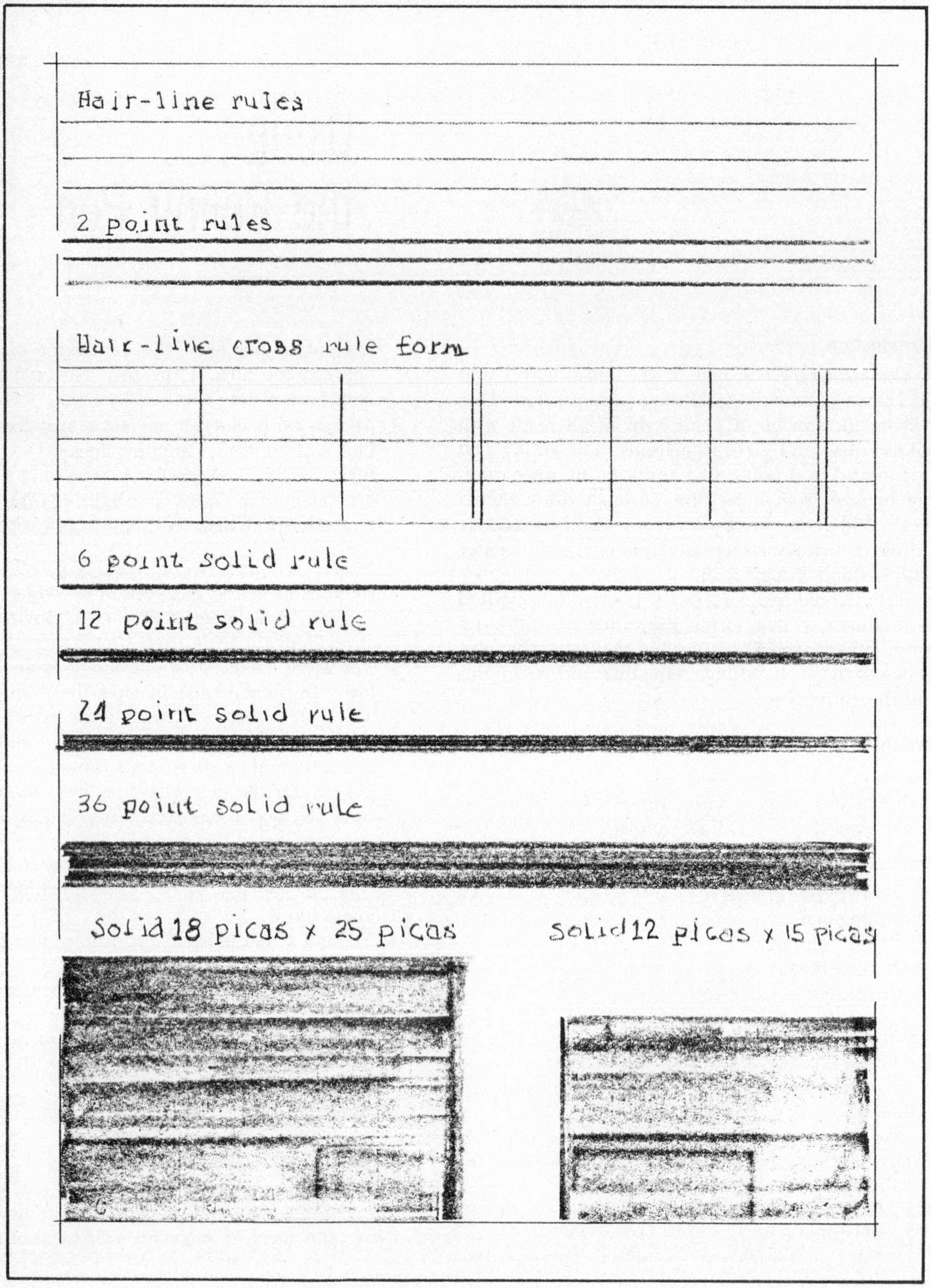

Hair-line rules

2 point rules

Hair-line cross rule form

6 point solid rule

12 point solid rule

24 point solid rule

36 point solid rule

Solid 18 picas x 25 picas   Solid 12 picas x 15 picas

Simple
Cross-Rule Forms

Introduction

Preparing cross-rule forms by the letterpress method is done by either setting the form in type and cutting in rules, or by the use of a tabular broach machine. These and other methods, including linotype and Ludlow were satisfactory for letterpress printing. Since offset printing does not require metal type, the ruling pen has been finding increased use in preparing these types of forms.

The student should develop the ability to rule evenly spaced lines of uniform thickness. This lesson emphasizes the need for uniformity of spacing between lines.

Words to Know

Tabular broach
Mortise

Materials Required

1. Basic paste-up tools
2. Ruling pen
3. Black India ink
4. Print trimmer

Procedure and Details

1. Outline a paper area of 5½″ × 8½″, with an image area of 5″ × 8″.
2. Type COPY A and COPY B, using a VariTyper or a standard typewriter. (You may substitute the heading from a readily available business form, if you like.)
3. On a separate sheet of paper, rule out the form, as shown in the rough layout.
4. Cut out a box and mortise in the column heads, from behind with Scotch tape.
5. Carefully trim the right and left hand margins of the form to create a perfect alignment of the rules.
6. Paste the rule form down in position as shown in the rough layout.
7. Paste down the heading as shown.
8. Cover the finished art with a protective cover.

Supplementary Reading

Polk: *The Practice of Printing*, Chap. 21 (Composition of Tabular Forms)

COPY A

```
   Offset                      Letterpress
         YOUR NAME PRINTING CO.
            Your Home Address
            Your City and State
               Your Phone
```

COPY B
```
Quantity   Description    Unit    Total
```

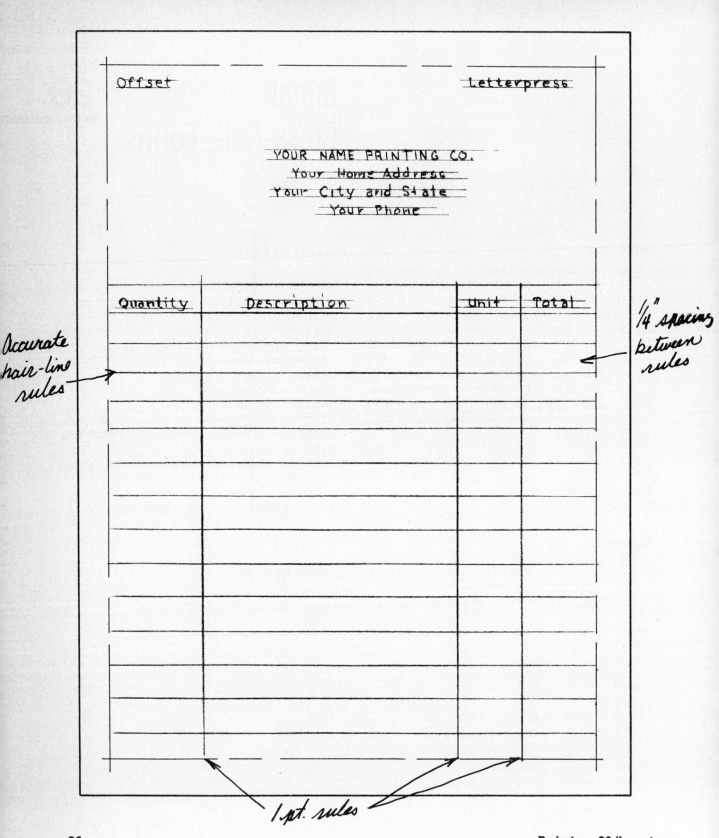

Offset   Letterpress

YOUR NAME PRINTING CO.
Your Home Address
Your City and State
Your Phone

Quantity	Description	Unit	Total

Accurate hair-line rules

¼" spacing between rules

1 pt. rules

Complex Cross-Rule Forms

Introduction

This lesson explores two different methods of preparing the same rule form. In one, the text is typed on a VariTyper or ordinary typewriter, and the ruling is done last. In the second method the form is first ruled completely, and the text is typed and cut in later. Each method will produce a satisfactory form. Each method has its advantages and disadvantages when related to a specific problem. The object of this lesson is to attempt the same form by both methods, and let the student draw his own conclusions as to which method he prefers.

Materials Required

1. Basic paste-up tools
2. Ruling pen
3. Black India ink
4. VariTyper, or standard typewriter

Procedure and Details

1. Outline a 6″ × 9″ paper area, with a 5½″ × 8½″ image area, on a piece of paper.
2. Complete a paste-up of the rule form shown in the rough layout. Type all of the text in its final position, as shown. After the typing is complete, draw in the rules around the typewritten material.
3. Complete another paste-up of the same rule form on translucent paper, this time ruling in the form first, and cutting in the heads later.
   You may use any of these methods to cut in the heads:
   a. Cut out the word to be inserted, and paste it down in position, carefully aligning it with a T square.
   b. Cut out a small window where the word is to appear and then tape the word in position from behind.
   c. Align the word to be inserted over the desired position in the paste-up. Do this over a light table. Carefully cut out a small window, cutting through both the sheet with the word and the blank underneath. Separate the two pieces of paper. Place a piece of Scotch tape behind the window on the form. Remove the word from the sheet, and press it down in the proper position over the tape.
4. Mount the finished paste-ups on illustration board.
5. Cover each paste-up with a protective cover.
6. Draw a conclusion as to which method was easier to complete. Would your conclusion hold true if there were a large number of inserts?

YOUR COMPANY NAME JOB TICKET

Customer's Name _____

Address _____

Date _____ Telephone _____

	Item 1	Item 2	Item 3
Descripition			
Quantity			
Size			
Stock			
Ink			
Pad			
Punch			
Perforate			
No. from			
Collate			
Shipping			
Price			

Amount $ _____

Proof _____   Tax $ _____

Date Promised: Total $ _____

_____   Deposit $ _____

Balance $ _____

Salesman _____   P.O. No. _____

Pressure Sensitive Tape

Introduction

A variety of pressure sensitive tapes are available which can be applied directly to artwork. The tapes come in many patterns, including solid lines, broken lines, stripes, crosshatch patterns, etc. The tapes come in rolls of various widths, from under 1/16″ to over 1/2″. An adhesive coating on the back of the tape facilitates applying them to artwork.

These tapes can be used to prepare column charts, bar graphs, line charts, organization charts, plant and office layouts, etc.

To use the tape, unwind the desired length, press it onto the illustration board and burnish it into position on the artwork. Some tapes are available in plastic dispensers which enable them to be applied directly to the artwork with a minimum of handling.

A blue guideline should be drawn on the artwork to facilitate aligning the tape before burnishing it down into position. All tapes should be burnished to be sure they are permanently bonded to the paste-up. A blunt, smooth instrument does a satisfactory job.

Simple line charts and bar graphs can be made using a single tape pattern. More complex charts are made using two or more patterns. Pressure sensitive tapes are a convenient way to apply boxes, borders, panels, etc.

Words to Know

Bar graph
Line chart
Burnish

Materials Required

1. Basic paste-up tools
2. Pressure sensitive tapes in various patterns and widths
3. Ruling pen
4. Black India ink

Procedure and Details

1. Outline an image area of 8″ × 10″, on a piece of illustration board, 8½″ × 11″.
2. Using light blue pencil, rule out the bar graph and line chart, as shown in the rough layout.
3. Rule in baseline and vertical line with India ink.
4. Using pressure adhesive letters, or other method to set text copy, insert the text and title as shown in the illustration.
5. Apply ¼″ solid rule to create the bar graph shown in the figure. Be sure the ends of the tapes are trimmed square and each bar is parallel.
6. Apply three different patterns of pressure sensitive tapes to the line chart, shown in the illustration. Follow the pattern and place the tapes on the art to form the curves as illustrated. After applying the tapes, burnish them securely to the artwork.
7. Cover the finished paste-up with a protective cover.

Supplementary Reading

Cogoli: *Photo-Offset Fundamentals*, Chapter 5 (Type Composition for Reproduction)

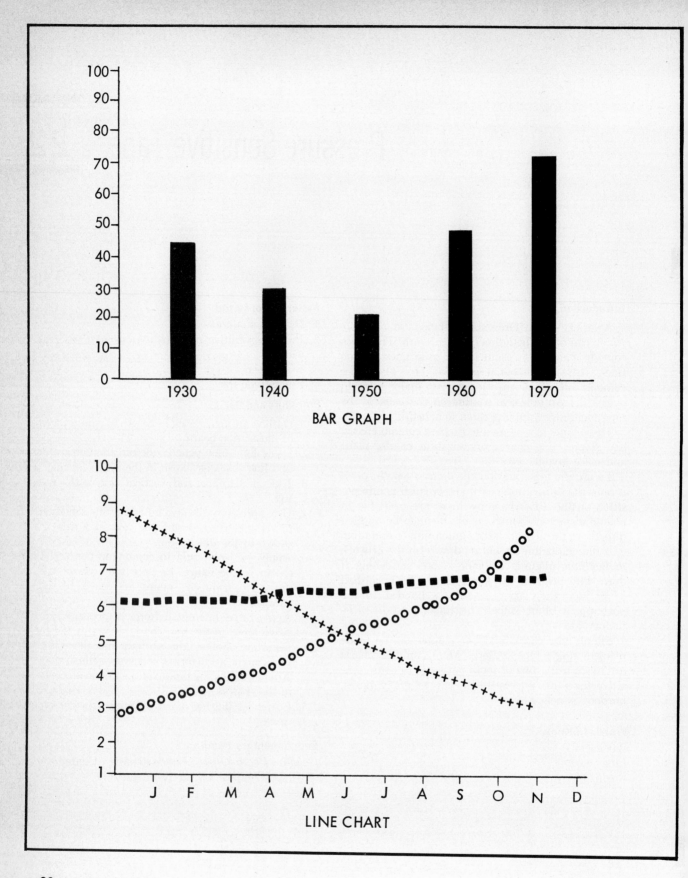

BAR GRAPH

LINE CHART

Market Display Advertisement

Introduction

Grocery stores and supermarkets often use newspapers, leaflets and direct mail pieces as promotional advertising. These ads include text in boxes, bordered copy, illustrations and large display prices. Paste-ups for these jobs require that a large amount of copy and illustrations be placed in a relatively small area. To facilitate pasting up, it is often best to work oversize and then reduce down for final printing.

The secret in designing these jobs is careful planning and use of available space. Since much copy, illustrations, boxes and text must be placed in the ad, it is essential that each element be planned to fit exactly.

Before beginning the paste-up, the artist should execute a carefully done layout, indicating the position of all elements of copy. Then blue pencil guidelines should be drawn on the illustration board to locate each piece of copy, border, box, etc. Finally the large display letters are pasted down, copy inserted into the boxes and text and proofs pasted down.

Words to Know

Display advertisement
Bordered copy

Materials Required

1. Basic paste-up tools
2. Proofs of newspaper display advertisements
3. Ruling pen and black India ink
4. Pressure sensitive tapes

Procedure and Details

1. Outline a 15″ × 21″ image area on a piece of illustration board, 16″ × 24″.
2. Following a carefully prepared layout, rule in the appropriate guidelines for all boxes, borders, rules, etc., in light blue pencil.
3. Use black India ink to draw rules and boxes. Apply pressure sensitive tapes for bordered boxes.
4. Trim proofs and paste them into the boxes and other areas where text is to be placed. Paste large display lettering in place.
5. Cover the finished paste-up with a protective cover.

Supplementary Readings

Ballinger: *Layout*
Cogoli: *Photo-Offset Fundamentals,* Page 81
Arnold: *Ink on Paper,* Chap. 19 (Layout)
Turnbull: *Graphics of Communication,* Chap. 15 (Newspaper Typography and Make-up)

shopping is a breeze at:

Jordan's

Shop & $ave

Produce - fresh daily

19¢ LB
Navel Oranges

HONEYDEW MELONS

17¢

CUCUMBERS
12¢ *lb*

SWEET CORN
17¢ *lb*

FRESH CRISP HEAD **LETTUCE**

24 SIZE
10¢ *lb*

POTATO CHIPS

so good

Hudson's canned

HAM COOKED BONELESS

8 lb $674

Right reserved to limit quantities

J. Pinkney
TWIN PACK
18 oz box
69¢

100 PAPER PLATES
9" wide
58¢
Why pay 71?

ALUMINUM FOIL 25 ft roll	CATSUP 14-oz btl
19¢ Why pay 26?	**18¢** Why pay 27?

BEVERAGES		FROZEN FOOD		SANDWICH MEAT		DAIRY PRODUCTS	
SQUELCHES 46-oz GRAPE DRINK	21¢	TASTI 2 lb CRINKLE CUT FRIES	65¢	GOLDS 8-oz pkg CHOPPED HAM	87¢	GOLDEN PRIDE 32-oz ORANGE JUICE	75¢
VITA COLA 6 12-oz cans COLA	79¢	EASY TIME 8-oz TURKEY POT PIES	35¢	GOLDS 8-oz can HAM & CHEESE	99¢	SCHLAGENHEIM 1 lb MARGARINE	3/79¢
GREGOR'S Fifth VODKA	$3.45	MA GOOGE 10-oz BROCCOLI SPEARS	2/99¢	LANCELOT'S 6-oz COOKED HAM	$1.05	STUNKARD 8-oz SWISS CHEESE	69¢
BARNHISEL 6 12-oz cans BEER	$1.09	MA GOOGE 10-oz PEAS & CARROTS	3/99¢	THOMPSON 10 lb SALAMI	76¢	JORDAN'S Dozen EGGS	50¢

Jordan's Grocery

Justifying Lines on a Typewriter

Introduction

There are occasions when an ordinary typewriter may be used to compose justified material. Justified material has both right and left margins in perfect alignment. While this may be done on an ordinary typewriter, the results are not as satisfactory as on a machine designed for that purpose. The quality of typewriter justification may be satisfactory for some applications, however.

Justification on these machines is accomplished by typing all material twice. First, a line is typed and the number of characters over or under the predetermined column width is indicated. The carriage is then moved over to a second column, and the line retyped, with space being added in or taken out, as necessary. Since all copy is typed twice, this method is time consuming on large amounts of text. The unjustified column, however, may be used for cutting corrections into the second column.

Materials Required

1. Basic paste-up tools
2. Standard typewriter

Procedure and Details

1. Outline a paper area of 5″ × 11″, with an image area of 4″ × 10″, on a piece of illustration board.

2. Type the material in COPY A, justifying the lines. Use the following procedure in typing the copy:
   a. Set the margins, and tabulator of the typewriter to produce two columns. Leave about five spaces between columns.
   b. Begin typing, and complete the first line. If the line is short two or three spaces, fill out the column with a series of ///. If the line is over by a character or two, type these into the margin.
   c. Move the carriage to the second column. Retype the line just completed. If the first line was short by a space or two, add these spaces at the most suitable points during the second typing. If the line was over, remove space from the second typing. The half-backspace may be helpful here.
   d. After completing the retype of the first line, go on to the second line. Continue until all material has been composed.
   e. After typing, proofread the copy. Use the first column as a source of corrected words. Cut these into the second column.
3. Paste the corrected second column in the center of the image area.
4. Cover the completed paste-up with a protective cover.

EXAMPLE OF JUSTIFICATION

All of the lines must be typed twice in order to make both the/ right and left hand margins even. If a letter goes out in the mar- gin, space must be taken out. If a line is short, space must be// added.

All of the lines must be typed twice in order to make both the right and left hand margins even. If a letter goes out in the mar- gin, space must be taken out. If a line is short, space must be added.

COPY A

JUSTIFYING ON A TYPEWRITER

While it may appear at first that the spacing of typewriter composition is satisfactory, closer observation will show that it is not as good as book composition. This is because the spacing is too uneven and un- pleasant to the eye. Good typography dictates that there be even and bal- anced spacing between words. This is difficult to accomplish when typing lines on an ordinary typewriter, since only the full space and half- space are available to the operator.

The compositor has available to him many more degrees of spacing than just the full space and half-space. Therefore, a compositor may alter the spacing in each line imperceptibly to create justified columns of pleas- ing appearance.

The typewriter method of justifi- cation is satisfactory when a low cost method of copy preparation is required. With care, adequate jus- tification may be achieved. But it is extremely difficult to preserve a pleasing appearance.

25 IBM "Selectric" Composer

Introduction

There are several types of IBM "Selectric" composing machines in use, which produce cold type composition. The free standing IBM "Selectric" Composer and the IBM Magnetic Tape "Selectric" Composer (MT/SC), both produce cold type composition from a rapidly moving round type element.

The free standing composer resembles a "Selectric" typewriter, has a replaceable type element and a carbon ribbon mechanism. Each time a key is depressed, a letter image is formed on the page. The IBM MT/SC has a tape system which stores keystrokes on a reel of magnetic tape. Errors are corrected on the MT/SC by backspacing and retyping. This backs up the tape and corrects the error. After all copy has been keyboarded, the machine plays out a corrected draft, without requiring re-keyboarding.

Justified composition can be produced on either machine. The free standing composer requires typing each line twice, while on the MT/SC, only one typing of the text is necessary. Both machines will produce justified, flush left, flush right and centered lines.

Words to Know

IBM Free Standing Composer
IBM Magnetic Tape "Selectric" Composer, (MT/SC)
Flush right
Flush left
Centered composition
Justification

Materials Required

1. Basic paste-up tools
2. Illustration, or small line drawing
3. India ink and ruling pen
4. IBM "Selectric" Composer, or Magnetic Tape "Selectric" Composer

Procedure and Details

1. Outline a paper area, 8½" × 11" and an image area of 7½" × 10", on a piece of illustration board.
2. Type the three paragraphs of copy shown in the rough layout. Follow the instructions, composing one paragraph flush left, another with justified text and the last with centered copy.
3. Rule in the box, around Copy B, as shown in the Figure.
4. Compose the display line at the top of the paste-up, using self-adhesive lettering. Paste it in position on the paste-up.
5. Paste down the drawing as shown.
6. Paste down the paragraphs of text set on the composing machine.
7. Cover the finished paste-up with a protective cover.

Copy A. Set copy below, flush left, on 25 picas:

Make your choice printing...the challenging career. You will want to evaluate three very important factor before making this choice:

1. Determine your interests
2. What are your aptitudes?
3. What is the importance, scope and future of the printing industry?

Copy B. Set copy below, justified on 34 picas:

No other invention known to man has made as dynamic, remarkable and permanent a contribution to our society as has printing. For this noble art, which had its beginning in the middle of the 15th century, has preserved the vast heritage of ideas of the early scholars, thinkers, artists and poets. Much of the creative genius of da Vinci, Shakespeare, Rousseau, Franklin and others would have been lost to the disappearing sands of time had it not been for printing. Our very social foundation is built directly on the ideas and laws set down by great minds, and preserved for us through the permanence cf the printed word.

Copy C. Set copy below, centered, 34 picas:

The Graphic Arts Industry needs
trained young men and women with skills.
The better trained student will find
a satisfying career in Graphic Arts.
Training is the key to success in the industry.

Supplementary Readings

Cogoli: *Photo-Offset Fundamentals,* Page 63
Karch: *Graphic Arts Procedures,* Page 196

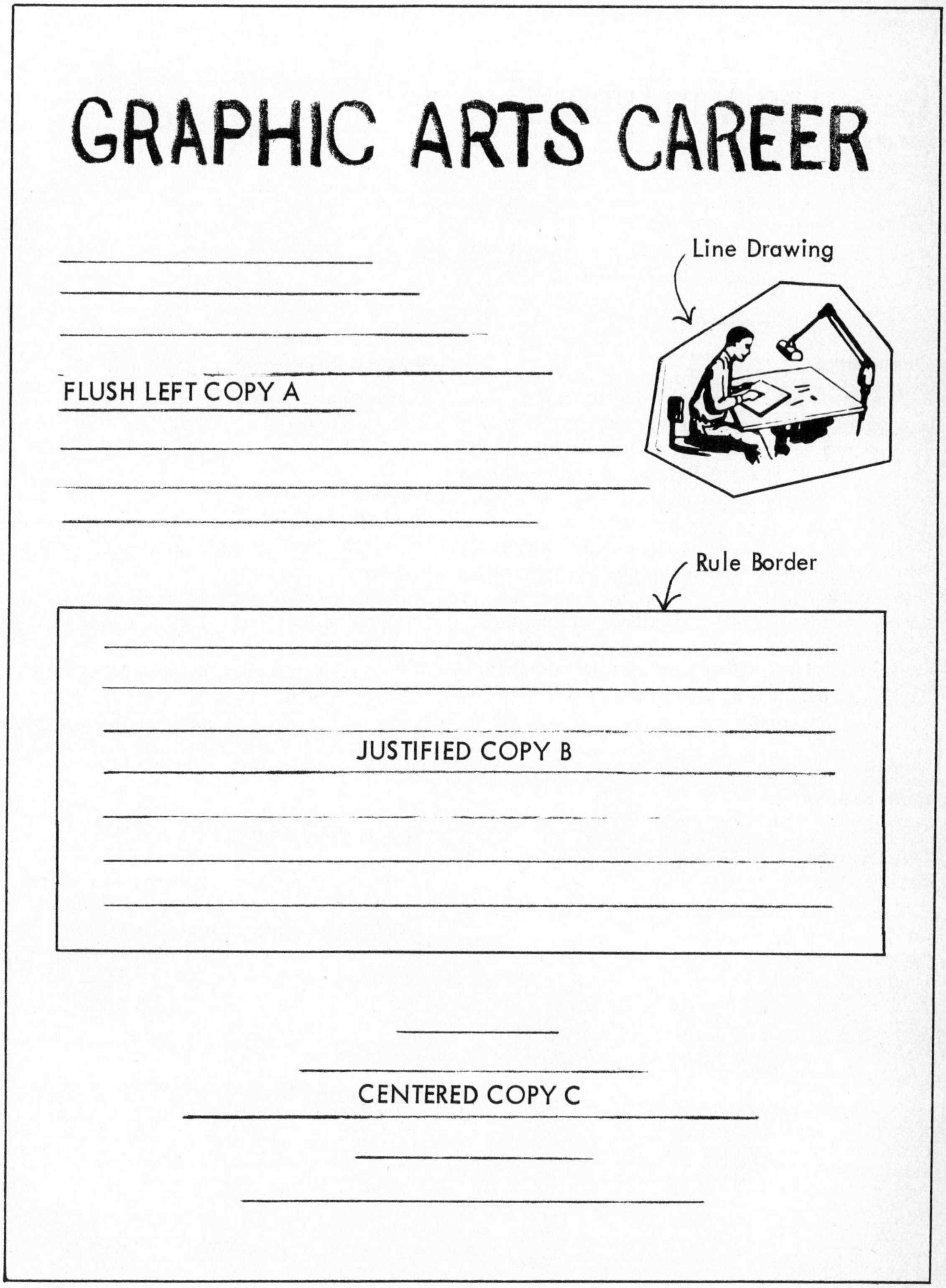

GRAPHIC ARTS CAREER

Line Drawing

_____
_____
_____
FLUSH LEFT COPY A
_____
_____
_____

Rule Border

_____
_____
_____
JUSTIFIED COPY B
_____
_____
_____

_____
CENTERED COPY C
_____
_____

26 The VariTyper

Introduction

The VariTyper is a device for producing cold-type composition for offset reproduction. It resembles an ordinary typewriter in appearance. It differs in that it is more flexible than an ordinary typewriter and uses a carbon instead of a linen ribbon.

The operator may easily change the typeface by inserting different type fonts. He can change the letterspacing and line spacing by simple adjustments. Some models will allow semi-automatic justification if the line is typed twice. An automatic horizontal ruling key may be obtained to facilitate making rule forms. This lesson explores a few of the many composition features of the VariTyper.

Words to Know

Composition
Letterspacing
Line spacing
Justification
Font
Strike-on image
Cold type

Materials Required

1. Basic paste-up tools
2. A VariTyper

Procedure and Details

1. Outline a paper area of $8\frac{1}{2}'' \times 11''$, and an image area of $7\frac{1}{2}'' \times 10''$, on a piece of illustration board.
2. Type the four paragraphs of copy in COPY A below, following the instructions given with each paragraph.
3. Paste down the four paragraphs as shown in the rough layout.
4. Cover the finished paste-up with a protective cover.

Supplementary Readings

Cogoli: *Photo-Offset Fundamentals,* Page 65
Cleeton-Pitkin: *General Printing,* Unit 107 (New Methods of Copy Composition)
Karch: *Graphic Arts Procedures—Basic,* Chap. 5 (How to Set Cold Type)

(12 pt. font, 10 letters per inch,
justify right and left margins, 30
pica column measure.)

The printing industry has created
a host of new employment opportunities for women. Modern printing
plants do not have the heavy lifting,
poor lighting and dirty plant facilities of the past. Printing has
expanded into areas which require the
craftsmanship which women have shown
in electronics and other areas.

(10 pt. font, 14 letters per inch,
justify right and left margins, 24
pica column measure.)

Lithography, a method of printing
which does not require handling heavy
metal forms, has created many excellent positions for women. Camera
work, strip-in, artwork, paste-up,
layout and design, are only a few of
the many jobs in this field available
to women. Salaries paid to women in
the field of lithography rank with
those paid to men, and even surpass
them in some specialized areas.

(12 pt. font, 10 letters per inch,
flush left and ragged right margin,
24 pica column measure.)

Young women looking for a career
today can find few occupations which
will pay as well and offer as many
benefits. Vacations, working conditions and salaries found in this
field make lithography a choice area
for the career minded young woman.
Yet few avail themselves of these
opportunities because of the outdated
concept that "only men are printers!"

(8 pt. font, 14 letters per inch,
justify right and left margins, 45
pica column measure.)

If you are a young woman looking
for a well-paying career with excep-
tional opportunity, look no further.
You will find a rewarding career with
a bright future in a modern industry
...Lithography.

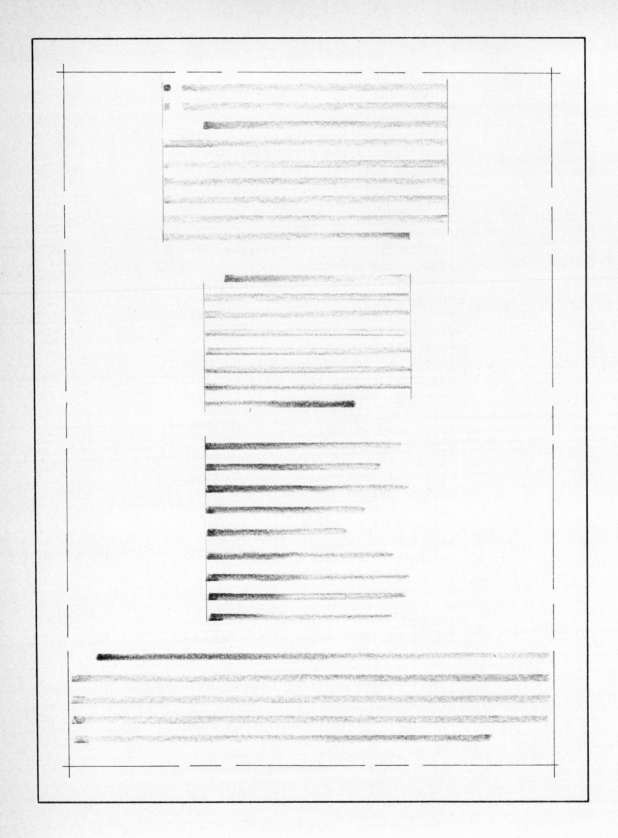

The Headliner

Introduction

The Headliner is representative of a large group of devices designed to produce finished lettering without setting type and pulling proofs. The lettering is produced photographically on print paper or transparent film. A simple device that uses a manually positioned negative master and a hand-held light source is one variety. Models are also available that automatically position the negative master, control the exposure and process the print strip. The Headliner will position, expose and process a strip of 35 mm (millimeter) photographic print paper or transparent film automatically.

These devices find wide use in setting headings and display copy. With an automatic model the operator simply dials the desired letter, depresses the exposure button, and the print is made. Next, the paper advances through a developer and fixer stage. The finished paper strip is allowed to dry and is then pasted down on the artwork. This lesson explores some of the applications of the Headliner.

Words to Know

Negative master
Exposure
Display line
Shading screen
Typemaster

Materials Required

1. Basic paste-up tools
2. A Headliner machine or similar device
3. Shading screens

Procedure and Details

1. Outline a paper area of $8\frac{1}{2}'' \times 11''$, and an image area of $7'' \times 10''$, on a piece of illustration board.
2. Set COPY A below, on the Headliner, or similar machine, and paste it down on the artwork as shown on the rough layout.
3. Cover the finished paste-up with a protective cover.

Supplementary Readings

Cogoli: *Photo-Offset Fundamentals*, Page 73

COPY A
(72 pt. Caps)

DISPLAY COPY

(72 pt. Caps and lower case, letterspace)

Letterspace

(48 pt. Caps, Insert screen to produce screened letters)

FLEXIBILITY

(60 pt. Caps and lower case, justified right and left margins, set on a 7" wide column.)
Charts are available which will help in setting material which is justified on both margins.

DISPLAY COPY

Letterspace

FLEXIBILITY

Charts are available which will help in setting material which is justi-fied on both margins

Halftone Finishes

Introduction

Lithographic halftones and photoengravings may be finished in a number of ways other than the conventional or "square" finish. The square finish is the most economical, and most frequently ordered. For some applications, however, other finishes may be desirable.

Outline halftones are those from which the surplus background material has been cut away, leaving only the central object. The dot pattern drops off following the contour of the object.

Vignette halftones are similar to outline halftones, except that the dots fade out into the background, rather than drop off sharply.

Highlight halftones are used to accentuate certain elements in the photograph, by adding brilliant highlights. These are accomplished artificially by removing some of the dots from these areas, permitting more of the white background to show through.

Inset Halftones are those which have more than one illustration included in the area of a larger illustration. Insets are often used to show enlarged views of a subject, and are usually placed in a spot that does not contain essential material.

Overprinting is often used to superimpose copy over an illustration. It is achieved by making two exposures. The first contains the halftone. The second exposure, directly over the first, contains the copy.

This lesson studies the various halftone finishes in use.

Words to Know

Square finish halftone
Outline halftone
Vignette halftone
Highlight halftone
Inset halftone
Overprinting

Materials Required

1. Basic paste-up tools
2. Specimens of various halftone finishes

Procedure and Details

1. Outline a 9″ × 12″ paper area, with an 8½″ × 11″ image area, on a piece of illustration board.
2. Using adhesive lettering, set the words "HALFTONE FINISHES" on a piece of paper and paste it down in the position shown on the rough layout.
3. Cut out the six halftone specimens required from the sheet included in this project. Paste them down in the position indicated on the layout.
4. Using a VariTyper or standard typewriter, type and insert the description below each specimen as illustrated.
5. Cover the finished paste-up with a protective cover.

Supplementary Readings

Turnbull: *The Graphics of Communication,* Chap. 6 (Plates for Letterpress Printing)
Polk: *The Practice of Printing,* Chap. 37 (Letterpress Printing Plates)
Arnold: *Ink on Paper,* Chap. 11 (Printing Plates)
Cogoli: *Photo-Offset Fundamentals,* Chap. 9 (Halftone Photography)
Karch and Buber: *Graphic Arts Procedures—The Offset Processes,* Chap. 5 (Offset Photography)

HALFTONE FINISHES

Square halftone

Outline halftone

Highlight halftone

Vignette halftone

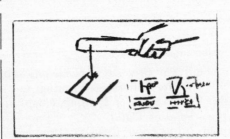

Inset halftone

Overprint halftone

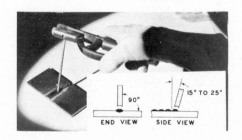

END VIEW   SIDE VIEW

90°   15° TO 25°

TRAFFIC

Handling Continuous Tone Photographs

Introduction

Continuous tone photographs are not suitable for inclusion with line material on the same paste-up. They require an additional step to break down the continuous tones into discrete areas of black and white. This process, called screening, yields what is called a halftone. It is necessary to separate all camera copy into two groups: line copy and continuous tone copy. This will facilitate the cameraman's work. All continuous tone copy should be "keyed" to the line material by using capital letters placed on the paste-up where the photo is to appear, and also by the photo. To further facilitate the cameraman's job, "windows" should be provided in the line negative to receive the proper illustration. This may be done by placing a piece of black paper on the line paste-up in the exact position that the photo will eventually appear. This will reproduce as a clear "window" on the negative. The screened halftone negative is then stripped in behind this window.

This lesson explores how to handle a paste-up which contains continuous tone photographs.

Words to Know

Halftone screen	Stripping
Continuous tone copy	Crop
Window	Highlight
Line negative	Middletone
Halftone negative	Shadow

Materials Required

1. Basic paste-up tools
2. Black paper

Procedure and Details

1. Outline a paper area of 8½″ × 11″, and an image area of 7½″ × 10″ on a piece of illustration board. Label this the "line flat."
2. Obtain another piece of illustration board, and label it "continuous tone flat."
3. With a ruling pen, rule a two point border around the job, as shown in the rough layout for the line flat.
4. Rule an 18 point × 36 pica line horizontally as shown.
5. Set and paste down the word PHOTOGRAPHS, using adhesive lettering.
6. Paste down a paragraph of 12 pt. copy as shown.
7. Carefully trim three pieces of black paper to the sizes shown on the rough layout. Paste these in the positions shown.
8. On the continuous tone flat, paste down the three photographs supplied here. You may trim these down to ¼″ larger than the windows, or indicate by crop marks the portions wanted.
9. Using light blue pencil, key the continuous tone photographs to their proper positions on the line flat using letters.
10. Cover both paste-ups with protective covers.

Supplementary Readings

Sayre: *Photography and Platemaking for Photo-Lithography*, Pages 279-302
Karch and Buber: *Graphic Arts Procedures—The Offset Processes*, Chap. 5 (Offset Photography)
Cogoli: *Photo-Offset Fundamentals*, Chap. 9 (Halftone Photography)
Eastman Kodak Company: *Basic Photography*

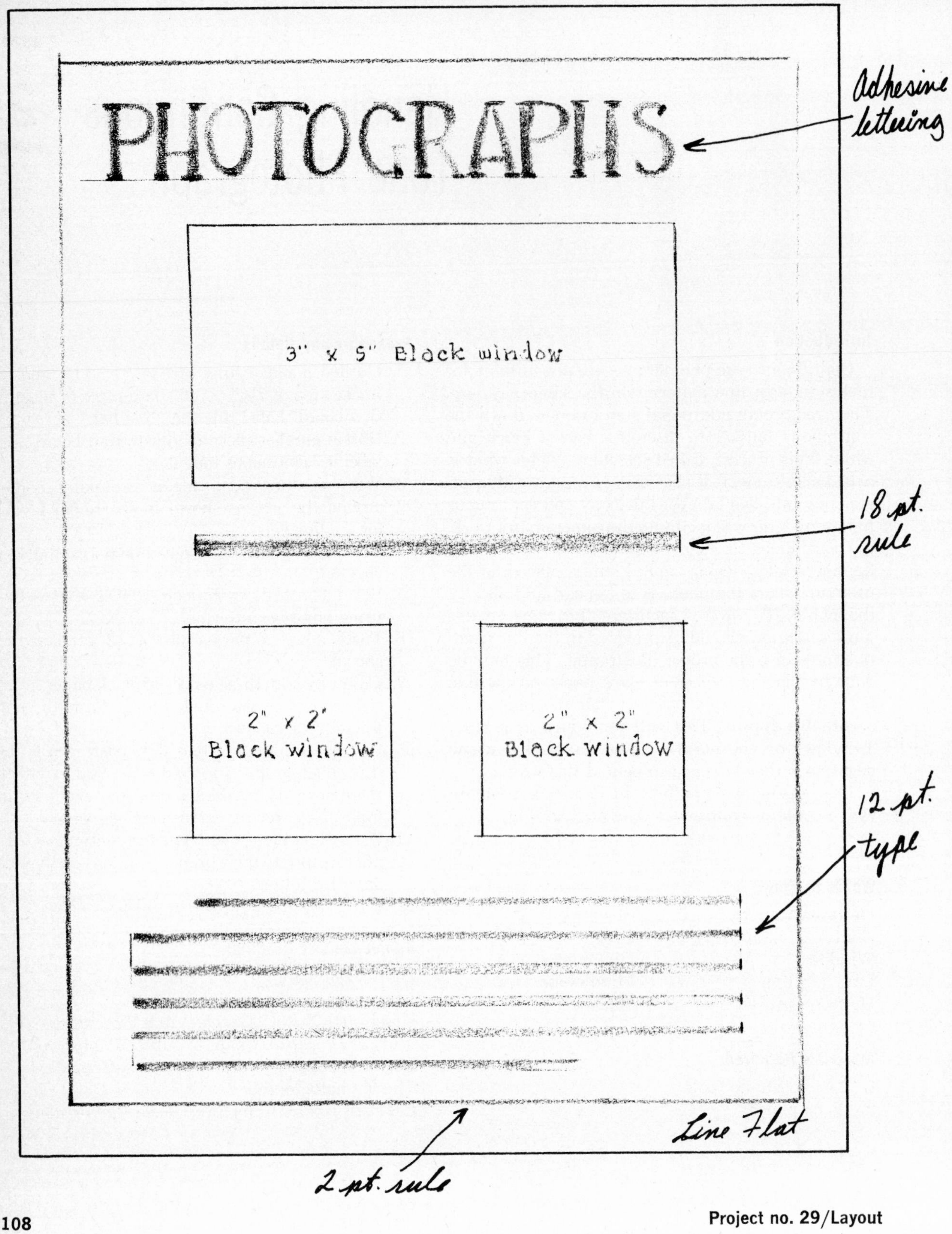

PHOTOGRAPHS

3" x 5" Black window

2" x 2"
Black window

2" x 2"
Black window

12 pt. type

Line Flat

2 pt. rule

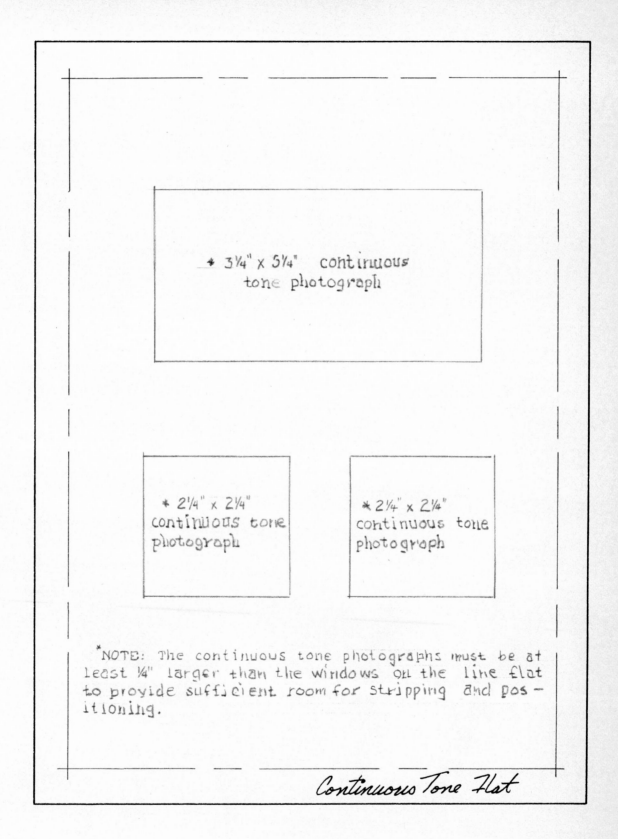

*NOTE: The continuous tone photographs must be at least ¼" larger than the windows on the line flat to provide sufficient room for stripping and positioning.

Continuous Tone Flat

Since all copy printed by the offset process must be photographed, it is possible, at little extra cost to either enlarge or reduce the artwork. One point must be borne in mind, however, when illustrations are enlarged: imperfections are exaggerated. On the other hand, an illustration that is reduced has its imperfections diminished. Details in photographs that might be objectionable when enlarged two or three times, become imperceptible when reduced a like amount. It is advisable to group pictures of similar contrast and quality so that they may be shot as a group, thus reducing camera time and expense.

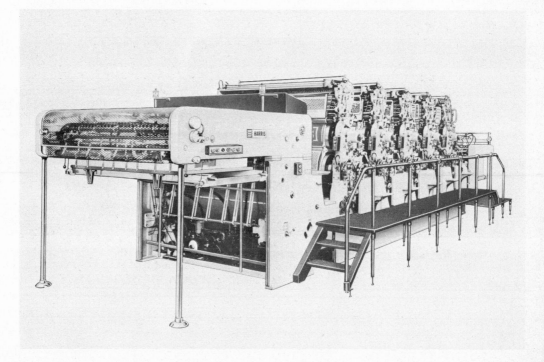

Scaling
Photographs and Copy

Introduction

This lesson will explore four methods of scaling photographs and copy. Much of the flexibility and advantage of working with a paste-up, is that it can be changed in size for the finished job. The artist should be able to calculate the new dimensions of any piece of work planned for a change in size. He may then determine, in advance, whether an illustration or piece of copy will fit in the desired area.

There are four common methods of figuring the new dimensions. They are (1) use of a proportion scale, (2) use of ordinary slide rule, (3) mathematical ratio and (4) diagonal method. The student should understand each of these in order to mark up copy properly and with the assurance that it will fit when changed in size.

Proportion Scale

This is a circular slide rule, with two dials. To find the *proportions* of a new size, line up one dimension of the original copy with the corresponding dimension of the new size. Other dimensions will line up around the dial. To find the percentage of reduction, the original size on the inner scale is lined up with the new size on the outer scale. The percentage of reduction shows in window on the scale. Most proportion scales give detailed instructions for use, and should be followed. The advantage of the proportion scale is that the *percentage of enlargement or reduction* as well as the *proportions* can be easily found.

Slide Rule

The common slide rule will be found useful in determining new sizes after reduction or blow-up. Essentially a slide rule is the same device as a proportion scale. The scale is etched in a linear or ruler form. The disadvantage of the slide rule is that it does not give the percentage of reduction in the window. To find the new size of a piece of copy, line up the original dimensions on the A and B scales. All new dimensions will line up accordingly. Move the slide along the scale to find the new width and depth.

Mathematical Ratio

The new size can be easily determined by a simple mathematical formula. No slide rule or proportion scale is necessary. To find the new size, substitute in the formula below:

$$\frac{\text{original width}}{\text{increased or decreased width}} = \frac{\text{original height}}{\text{increased or decreased height}}$$

EXAMPLE: Suppose a photograph 8″ x 10″ is to be reduced to 4″ wide. What will be the new depth?

$$\frac{8''}{4''} = \frac{10''}{x \ (?)''}$$

Cross multiply and then divide to find the value of x.

$$8x = 40$$
$$x = 5''$$

Diagonal Method

New sizes can be satisfactorily determined by means of a simple diagonal drawing. Proceed with the steps below. (See Figure 30-1)

a. Draw the size of the original illustration on a sheet of paper.

b. Draw a diagonal line from the bottom left corner of the illustration through the top right corner, and on out to the end of the sheet of paper.

c. Measure the new width of the illustration along the bottom (base line) of the original paper size.

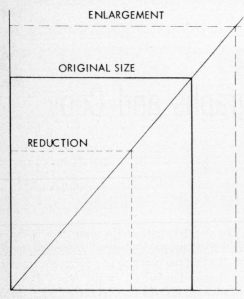

ENLARGEMENT

ORIGINAL SIZE

REDUCTION

FIGURE 30–1

Mark this point. Next draw a vertical line at right angles to the base line, up to the diagonal line.

d. At the point of intersection, draw a horizontal line to complete the rectangle. The area marked by the rectangle you have just drawn will be the new size.

It should be remembered that a piece of copy can only be reduced, or blown up in proportion. The new relationship of width to depth will always be in the same ratio at the old relationship. Thus a large, *narrow* area will always reduce to a small, *narrow* area. It is not possible to reduce it to a small, *wide* area. This is because the camera lens always acts to reduce both width and depth in proportion. The exception to this is to use a distortion prism on the camera lens. It is then possible to change the proportions of the original by distorting the camera copy. This feature is not normally available on process cameras.

Words to Know

Proportion
Proportion scale
Blow-up
Reduction
Mathematical ratio

Materials Required

1. Basic paste-up tools
2. Proportion scale
3. Slide rule
4. Ruler

Procedure and Details

1. Remove the proof with the three illustrations. Paste each of these on an 11″ × 14″ piece of illustration board. Cover with a translucent overlay.
2. The present size of Photograph A is 3″ × 3″, B is 1″ × 3½″ and C is 4¼″ × 6¾″. Calculate the following sizes, and percentages, and record these in light blue pencil on the overlay.

a. Using the proportion scale, determine the percentage of reduction, if Photo A were reduced to 1¾″ × 1¾″.

b. Using the diagonal method, determine the new width, if Photo B were blown-up to 10″ deep.

c. Using the proportion scale, determine the new sizes of Photo A, B, and C, if all were reduced 60%.

d. Using the diagonal method, calculate the new size, if Photo C were reduced to 2″ wide.

e. Using the slide rule, calculate the new width, if Photo C were reduced to 3″ deep.

Supplementary Readings

Arnold: *Ink on Paper,* Chap. 11 (Printing Plates)
Cogoli: *Photo-Offset Fundamentals,* Chap. 7 (Preparing Camera Copy for Reproduction)
Turnbull: *The Graphics of Communication,* Chap. 13 (Copy for the Photoengraver and Lithographer)

PHOTO A

PHOTO B

PHOTO C

Cropping Photographs

Introduction

It is often neither practical nor possible to cut a large photograph down in order to show what part is wanted. Cropping is the method used by lithographers and artists to indicate which portion is desired, without actually marking across or cutting the photograph. Two methods are commonly used. One is marginal marking, and the other is overlay marking. Both permit the illustration to be used again and are explored here.

Words to Know

Crop marks
Overlay

Materials Required

1. Basic paste-up tools
2. Sheet of translucent tracing paper
3. China marking pencil

Procedure and Details

1. Crop the photograph supplied here, using both methods. First, use the marginal marking method. Using a T square and a China marking pencil, mark two sets of horizontal lines in the side margins, indicating the desired area. Mark two sets of vertical lines in the top and bottom margins. These marks should be only in the margins, and not on the photograph proper. Crop marks may be easily removed for future recropping.
2. Mount a sheet of translucent overlay material over the photograph. Carefully mark the area to be cropped as shown on the rough layout. Be sure to make your marks on the overlay and not on the photograph itself.
3. Paste the photograph, together with the overlay, on a piece of illustration board to keep it flat.
4. Cover the entire paste-up with a protective cover.

Supplementary Readings

Turnbull: *The Graphics of Communication,* Chap. 13 (Copy for the Photoengraver and Lithographer)
Arnold: *Ink on Paper,* Chap. 11 (Printing Plates)

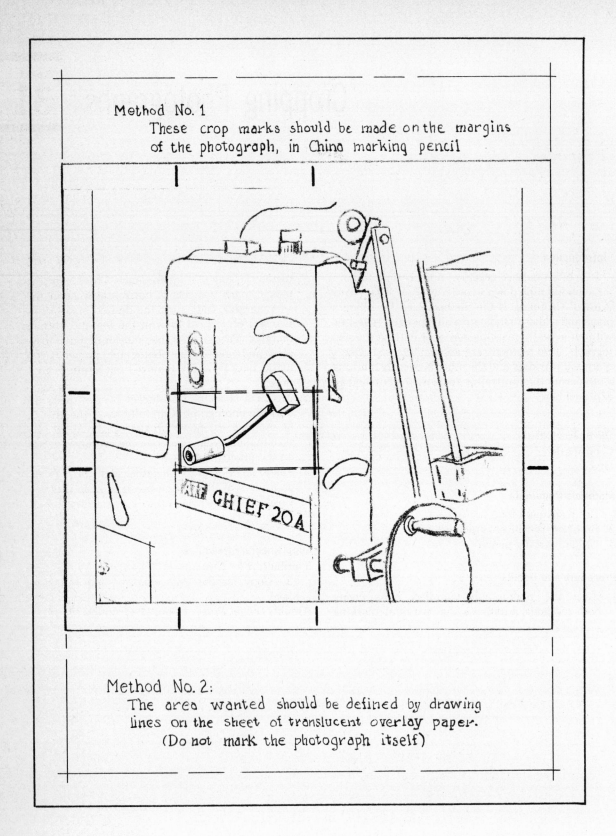

Method No. 1
   These crop marks should be made on the margins
of the photograph, in China marking pencil

CHIEF 20A

Method No. 2:
   The area wanted should be defined by drawing
lines on the sheet of translucent overlay paper.
(Do not mark the photograph itself)

The Color Wheel

Introduction

An understanding of the color wheel is fundamental to the artist or lithographer who works with color. By means of this device, he may create and plan jobs that use color harmoniously.

Color has three dimensions: *Hue,* the name of the color; *Value,* the degree of lightness or darkness; and *Chroma,* the measure of intensity of a color. More elaborate systems may illustrate all three dimensions.

When planning any color job, color harmony is important. Four relationships should be observed to obtain a harmonious choice of colors.

a. Monochromatic color harmony: Shades and tints of one hue.

b. Analogous color harmony: Adjacent colors are said to be in analogous color harmony.

c. Complementary color harmony: Two colors opposite each other on the color wheel are said to be in complementary color harmony.

d. Triadic color harmony: Three colors that form points of an equilateral triangle on the color wheel are in triadic color harmony.

The colors around the wheel from red through yellow are considered "warm" colors, while the colors from green through violet are considered "cold" colors.

Words to Know

Hue	Complementary color
Chroma	Triadic colors
Value	Analogous colors
Monochromatic color	

Materials Required

1. Basic paste-up tools
2. Tempera colors (Red, Orange, Yellow, Green, Blue and Violet)
3. Compass
4. Water color paper
5. Scissors
6. Sable brush

Procedure and Details

1. Draw two concentric circles on a piece of water color paper (Outer circle diameter 10″; and inner circle diameter 5″.
2. Paint in a band of red, yellow and blue, at the points of an equilateral triangle, as shown on the rough layout. Use tempera paint.
3. Paint in bands of orange, green and violet.
4. Using a brush and clear water, blend colors which are adjacent. Attempt to create a smooth, uniform transition from one color to the next.
5. After the colors have dried, cut out the wheel. Cut out the center.
6. Mount the wheel in the center of a piece of illustration board, using rubber cement.
7. Mount an overlay of translucent tracing paper over the wheel.
8. Cover the paste-up with a protective cover.
9. Using a soft pencil, mark the following color harmony details on the sheet of overlay paper.

   a. Draw a capital letter C over the color red. Draw a capital C over the opposite color on the wheel. These two represent a complementary color harmony.

   b. Draw a capital letter A over the color blue, and a capital A over the two adjacent colors. This is an example of analogous color harmony.

   c. Draw a capital letter T over the yellow, red and blue. These three represent triadic color harmony.

   d. Check off the colors around the wheel which are considered warm.

   e. Put x's by the colors around the wheel which are considered cold.

Supplementary Readings

Polk: *The Practice of Printing,* Chap. 31 (The Use of Color in Printing)

Turnbull: *The Graphics of Communication,* Chap. 14 (Color in Printing)

Arnold: *Ink on Paper,* Chap. 12 (Color Printing)

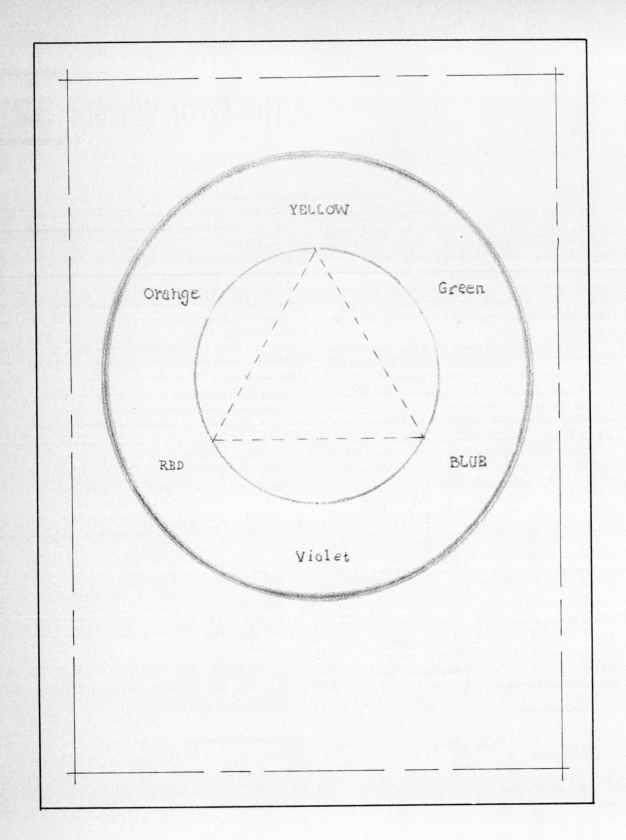

Using Register Marks

Introduction

Register marks are small, specially created designs which are placed on artwork, negatives or printing plates to control the accurate placement of one color over another. These marks find wide utility in paste-up work. They are applied to the illustration board and to the overlay material so that they align perfectly. Usually, a set of two register marks is placed on the illustration board, one mark in each of two diagonal corners. A set would also be placed on each overlay, so that they would fall directly on top of those on the board. On large paste-ups, a set of four marks might be used on the board and each overlay. Thus both pieces may be separated, worked on, and placed together again in the same position. Paste-ups for multicolor jobs should always contain a set of these marks for each overlay and the illustration board. This lesson will show the advantages of using register marks in paste-up work.

Words to Know

Positive register mark
Negative register mark

Materials Required

1. Basic paste-up tools
2. Wax-backed register marks
3. Sheet of clear acetate (.005" to .010" thick)
4. Ruling pen
5. Black India ink

Procedure and Details

1. Outline a paper area of $8\frac{1}{2}'' \times 11''$, and an image area of $7\frac{1}{2}'' \times 10''$, on a piece of illustration board.
2. Obtain a sheet of clear acetate $9'' \times 12''$. Center at the top only.
3. Place a set of two register marks on the illustration board. These should be in diagonal corners and close to, but outside of, the paper area. Note their position on the rough layout.
4. Place another set of register marks on the overlay, so that they align perfectly with those on the flat.

5. Complete the first part of the paste-up by pasting down the material below on the illustration board as shown on the rough layout.
   a. Cut apart and paste down the reproduction proof text.
   b. Obtain a line drawing and paste it down as shown.
   c. Paste down another line drawing as shown.
   d. Apply a $2'' \times 2''$ piece of 70% tint screen to flat as shown.
   e. Rule a 6 pt. vertical line in the position shown.
   f. Label the board "Blue Transparent Ink".
6. Complete the second part by pasting down the material below on the acetate overlay.
   a. Cut apart and paste down the headings from the reproduction proof which are to appear on the overlay.
   b. Paste down a $2'' \times 2''$ solid area over one line drawing as shown.
   c. Apply a piece of $2'' \times 2''$ textured tint screen over one line drawing as shown.
   d. Apply a $2'' \times 2''$ piece of 30% tint screen on the overlay over the 70% screen on the flat.
   e. Label the acetate overlay "Yellow Transparent Ink".
7. Cover the finished paste-up with a protective cover.
8. Use the Study Chart to determine which register marks would be best for each of the following applications.
   a. Use directly on flats and acetate overlays
   b. Use on positive film materials
   c. Use on negative film materials
   d. Use on material which will go from positive to negative

Supplementary Readings

U. S. Government Printing Office: *Theory and Practice of Lithography,* Chap. 2 (Negatives)

Cogoli: *Photo-Offset Fundamentals,* Chap. 12 (Laying Out and Stripping the Flat)

Sayre: *Photography and Platemaking for Photo-Lithography*

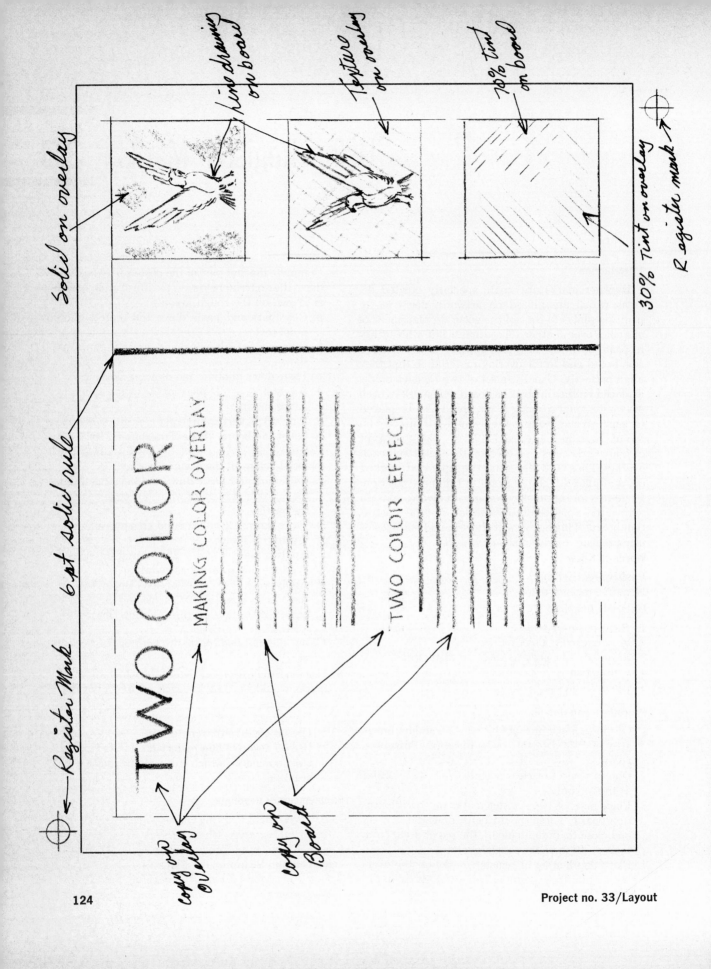

Line drawing on board

Texture on overlay

70% tint on board

30% tint overlay

Register mark

Solid on overlay

6 pt solid rule

Register Mark

TWO COLOR

MAKING COLOR OVERLAY

TWO COLOR EFFECT

copy on Overlay

copy on Board

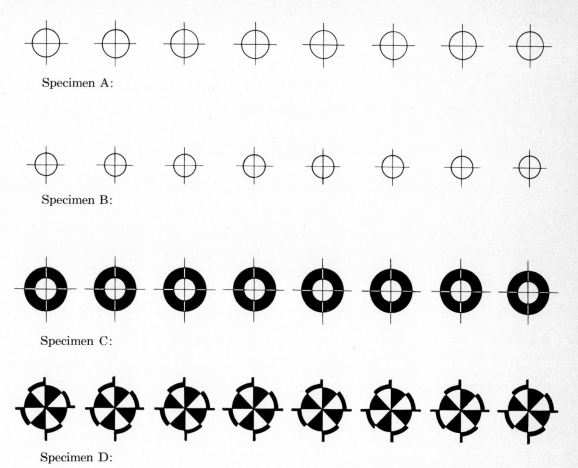

Specimen A:

Specimen B:

Specimen C:

Specimen D:

Explanation of Register Marks

Specimen A:

A standard register mark used on paste-ups. It is designed to be used in its positive form. It may be used on both illustration board, and overlays.

Specimen B:

A smaller version of the standard positive register mark above. It may be used where space is limited.

Specimen C:

A register mark for use with positive transparencies. These marks can be reproduced on film in either a positive or negative form. They are used for multi-color printing. Each segment of the circle appears in a different color.

Specimen D:

This is an alternate of the mark "C", above. It can be used in multi-color printing, in both positive and negative form.

TWO COLOR

From these two separate shots two offset plates would be prepared, and the job would then be printed. First the base color would be printed, being sure to hold close register on the press. Then the plate made from the overlay would be printed. This would be run in another color of ink, and again in exact position, so that the two colors would print in the proper relation. Thus the pattern of color break-up must be carefully followed so that any material to print on the base color must be pasted down on the base flat.

Many interesting two color effects may be created by using the overlay methods. For instance, it is possible to paste down a black square of paper on the paste up, and on the overlay, a line drawing could be pasted down. The final printed effect would be a line drawing printed over a solid color. Also a tint screen could be used instead of a solid color, and thus a line drawing would print over a screen background. Further, many interesting color combinations could be made by pasting down screens of different values on both the overlay and the base pasteup.

TWO COLOR EFFECTS

MAKING COLOR OVERLAY

Color Paste-Up I
Two Opaque Colors

Introduction

This lesson uses transparent acetate overlays as a method of preparing a two-color printing job. This method of separating the colors for each run is called mechanical color separation, since it is done by hand. An alternate method, called process color separation, relies on a camera to filter the colors apart.

The mechanically separated job will be printed in two steps. First the overlay will be photographed, a plate made, and a run completed in yellow ink. Next the base color will be photographed, a plate made, and a run completed in black ink, over the yellow.

The student should learn to think of the second color as an integral part of the layout. Use it to accent important copy, to establish a design axis, or create a unifying background effect. This lesson permits wide design latitude, and no rough layout is given. The student's judgment is relied upon for the successful use of the second color.

Words to Know

Mechanical color separation
Process color separation
Filter
Register marks

Materials Required

1. Basic paste-up tools
2. Sheet of clear acetate
3. Register marks
4. China marking pencil

Procedure and Details

1. Outline a paper area of 4″ × 10″ on a piece of illustration board.
2. Mount a sheet of clear acetate over the paper area. Secure the top only with masking tape.
3. Label the line flat "Black ink", and the overlay "Yellow ink".
4. Apply two sets of register marks in diagonal corners of the paste-up; one on the flat, the other on the overlay, just outside of the paper area.
5. Design a two-color layout, using black ink for the base color and yellow for the second color. (Note that all artwork will actually be done in black and white only!) Include the following design elements in the project:
   a. A Contemporary, off-center layout.
   b. Two paragraphs of copy.
   c. Approximately 8 square inches of solid color on the overlay. Integrate this into the design.
   d. A good choice of type styles, sizes, weights and spacing.
6. Complete the paste-up and cover it with a protective cover.

Supplementary Readings

Cogoli: *Photo-Offset Fundamentals*, Chap. 12 (Laying out and Stripping the Flat)
Turnbull: *The Graphics of Communication*, Chap. 14 (Color in Printing)
Karch and Buber: *Graphic Arts Procedures—The Offset Processes*, Chap. 5 (Offset Photography)

35 Color Paste-Up II
Three Opaque Colors

Introduction

This lesson deals with the combination of three colors on a printed piece. This requires careful consideration of the hue, amount and intensity of the colors as well as their juxtaposition. You may use any three colors you wish. However, you may want to review Project 32 before choosing.

Materials Required

1. Basic paste-up tools
2. Clear acetate sheets
3. China marking pencil
4. Register marks

Procedure and Details

1. Outline a paper area of 6″ × 9″, on a piece of illustration board.

2. Mount two sheets of clear acetate over the line flat. Secure both of these at the top with masking tape.

3. Using a China marking pencil, label each overlay and the illustration board for the ink colors of your choice.

4. Apply a set of two register marks in diagonal corners of the board and each overlay.

5. Design an off-center, using your three colors. Use any illustrations or text you wish. Be sure to consider carefully your choice of margins, white space and type styles. Make sure that some copy appears in each of the three colors.

6. Cover the finished paste-up with a protective cover.

Color Paste-Up III
Two Transparent Colors

Introduction

Transparent inks are those which blend together to produce a secondary color when they are printed one on top of the other. For example, printing a transparent blue over a transparent yellow ink will produce the color green.

It is therefore possible to plan combinations of the primary colors, using transparent inks to produce a variety of secondary colors. It is this blending effect which permits multicolor printing at low cost.

Some simple secondary combinations are as follows: red and yellow produce orange, red and blue produce violet, yellow and blue produce green. A study of the color wheel will suggest some of the many combinations which may be planned into the layout.

Materials Required

1. Basic paste-up tools
2. Clear acetate sheets
3. China marking pencil
4. Register marks

Procedure and Details

1. Outline a paper area of 7″ × 10″, on a piece of illustration board.
2. Mount a sheet of clear acetate over the paper area. Secure it at the top with masking tape.
3. Using a China marking pencil, label the illustration board and the overlay for two primary transparent ink colors of your choice.
4. Apply a set of two register marks in diagonal corners of the paste-up and also on the overlay, just outside of the paper area.
5. Design a layout, using two transparent primary colors. Use any illustrations or copy you wish. Be sure to consider carefully your choice of margins, white space and type styles. Use either an off-center or a center layout. See that some copy or illustrations appear in each color. Plan the layout to also include some copy in both colors that will blend to produce a new, secondary color.
6. Cover the finished paste-up with a protective cover.

Color Paste-Up IV
Three
Transparent Colors

Introduction

This project incorporates the use of three primary colors to produce several secondary colors. It gives the student the opportunity to use both primary and secondary colors in a layout. A carefully planned color scheme should be worked out before attempting to complete the layout.

Materials Required

1. Basic paste-up tools
2. Clear acetate sheets
3. China marking pencil
4. Register marks

Procedure and Details

1. Outline a paper area of 9″ × 12″, on a piece of illustration board.
2. Mount two sheets of clear acetate over the paper area. Secure both at the top with masking tape.
3. Using a China marking pencil, label the board "Transparent blue," one overlay "Transparent yellow" and the last overlay "Transparent red."
4. Apply three sets of register marks to diagonal corners of the paste-up just outside of the paper area, two marks on the illustration board and two on each of the overlays.
5. Design a three-color layout, using red, yellow and blue. Use any illustrations or copy you wish. Consider carefully your choice of margins, white space and type styles. Use either a center or off-center layout. See that some copy or illustrations appear in each of the transparent colors. Plan the layout to also include some copy in each of the secondary colors that will be produced.
6. Cover the finished paste-up with a protective cover.

Color Paste-Up V Imitation Duotone

Introduction

This lesson explores the imitation duotone. A true duotone is made by photographing continuous tone copy twice, each time at a different screen angle. These two shots are printed in different colors one on top of the other, to produce an interesting two-color picture. When a two-color effect is desired, but cost must be kept low, the imitation duotone technique may be helpful. Only one negative is made from the continuous tone original, and this is printed over a solid block of color. The background color will show through the halftone, producing a simulated duotone effect.

Materials Required

1. Basic paste-up tools
2. Clear acetate sheet
3. China marking pencil
4. Register marks
5. Black paper

Procedure and Details

1. Outline a paper area of 8¼″ × 11″, on a piece of illustration board.
2. Mount a sheet of clear acetate over the paper area. Secure it at the top with masking tape.
3. Using the China marking pencil, label the board "Black ink" and the overlay "Light blue ink."
4. Apply two sets of register marks in diagonal corners of the paste-up, just outside of the paper area.
5. Design a two-color layout, using black for the base color, and light blue as the second color. Include the following elements in the design:
   a. A center layout
   b. Two paragraphs of copy on the board
   c. A 20 square-inch halftone on the board
   d. A large display line on the board
6. After completing the paste-up of the base color, prepare the material for the overlay.
   a. Cut out a piece of black paper, exactly the size of the halftone photograph
   b. Paste this down on the overlay acetate, in the same position as the halftone photograph
7. Cover the finished paste-up with a protective cover.

COPY FOR PROJECT 38

A true duotone is produced by an interesting camera technique that produces a two-color printed picture. It is achieved by photographing an illustration twice, each time at a different screen angle. When the job is printed, the colors blend to create a pleasant visual effect.

The drawback of the true duotone is the fact that the illustration must be shot twice. It is possible to create an effect similar to a true duotone by shooting the illustration once and printing it over a block of solid color. The background color will show through and create an effect similar to a duotone that is easier and less expensive.

Hand Composition Paste-Up

Introduction

This lesson is a simple exercise in the elements of hand composition, coupled with a paste-up project. It involves setting type, proofing, distribution and paste-up. Flush left, centered and justified lines are explored.

Words to Know

Proof
Distribution
Flush left
Flush right
Center
Justification
Stick
Slug
Bearers
Reproduction proof

Materials Required

1. Basic paste-up tools
2. Hand composition facilities
3. Reproduction proof paper
4. Ruling pen
5. Black India ink

Procedure and Details

Part One (Setting flush left lines)

1. Obtain a composing stick and set it to 12 picas.
2. Place one slug space in the stick.
3. Set the following four lines. Begin with the letters set upside down, from left to right in the stick. After setting each line, space out the line to fill the stick. Keep the larger spaces on the inside of the line, and tilt the stick to see if the line is sufficiently tight.

COPY A:

```
YOUR NAME
YOUR ADDRESS
CITY AND STATE
TELEPHONE NUMBER
```

4. After setting all four lines, pull a proof on newsprint paper. Check it over for accuracy.
5. Once the proof has been corrected, pull three reproduction proofs. Use bearers around the form and a good grade of reproduction proof paper, inking the form carefully. Store these proofs for future use.
6. Distribute the type carefully. Put each character back in the proper place in the case. Be sure that spaces are replaced properly.

Part Two (Setting centered lines)

1. Obtain a composing stick and set it to 12 picas.
2. Place one slug space in the stick.
3. Set the following copy, centering each line. Any space added to one side must also be added to the opposite side of the line. Use caps and lower case.

COPY B:

```
Your first and last name
            Age
      Student number
        Address
    City and State
```

4. After setting all five lines, pull a proof on newsprint paper. Check it over for accuracy, correcting any errors.
5. Pull three proofs on reproduction proof paper. Store these for future use.
6. Distribute the type carefully.

Part Three (Setting justified material)

Justification is the process of spacing out a line of type so that it is aligned along both the right and left margin. This is done by carefully increasing or decreasing the space between words.

1. Set the following paragraph, on a 22 pica measure.

COPY C:

>   The Graphic Arts industry offers
> many excellent employment opportuni-
> ties to individuals who have advanced
> training. Technical advancements in
> the Graphic Arts are coming rapidly,
> and those students with college back-
> grounds are best able to understand
> and accept these changes. The
> Graphic Arts industry offers excel-
> lent employment conditions and oppor-
> tunities to individuals who are
> willing to study new methods and
> processes.

2. Pull a proof on newsprint paper, and check it for accuracy. Make any necessary corrections.
3. Pull three reproduction proofs. Store these for future use.

Part Four (Setting justified material)

1. Set the first 10 lines of the first paragraph of Chapter _____*, in the book _____*. Indent each paragraph one em quad.

2. Pull a proof on newsprint, and correct it.
3. Pull three reproduction proofs.

Part Five (Setting display matter)

1. Using a 36 point type on a 30 pica measure, set the copy below.

COPY D.

Your Name

2. Pull a proof on newsprint paper, check it for accuracy, and then pull three reproduction proofs. Store these for future use.

Part Six (Making the paste-up)

1. Outline a paper area of 8½″ × 11″, and an image area of 7½″ × 10″ on a piece of illustration board.
2. Gather together Copy A through D above, and complete a paste-up as shown on the rough layout.
3. Cover the finished paste-up with a protective cover.

Supplementary Readings

Polk: *The Practice of Printing*, Chap. 6 (The Process of Setting Type) and Chap. 7 (The Handling of Type Forms)

Cleeton-Pitkin: *General Printing*, Units 4-49

Turnbull: *The Graphics of Communication*, Chap. 4 (Type Measurement and Hand Composition)

Karch: *Graphic Arts Procedures—Basic,* Chap. 4 (How to Set "Hot" Type)

Carlsen: *Graphic Arts*, Chap. 2 (Fundamentals of Composition)

---

*Note: The instructor may wish to assign each student a different chapter so each can solve different spacing problems.

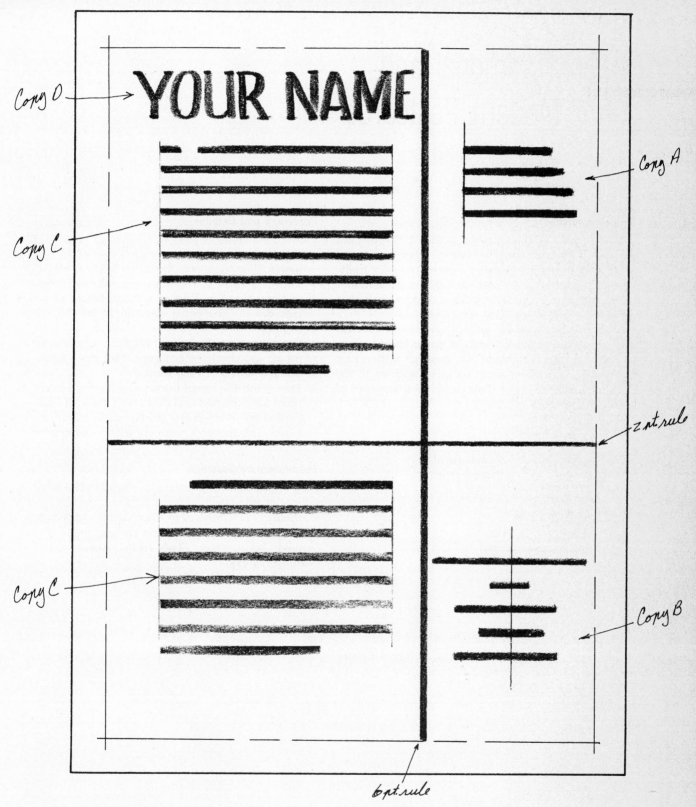

Copy D

Copy A

Copy C

Copy C

2 pt. rule

Copy B

6 pt. rule

YOUR NAME

Traditional and Modern Postcards

Introduction

The student should develop the ability to plan and create interesting layouts of either traditional or modern design. Usually, copy or text of a traditional nature appears best when it is in a traditional layout, and conversely, modern themes look best when a modern layout is employed.

With most modern subjects, copy and illustrations should be treated with off-center layouts. Traditional subjects should be handled with center layouts. Consideration should also be given to the correct choice of type. This lesson considers each of these principles.

Words to Know

Rough layout   Symmetrical
Axis   Asymmetrical

Materials Required

1. Basic paste-up tools
2. A 4B Charcoal pencil
3. Hand composition facilities

Procedure and Details

1. Design a series of modern thumbnail layouts of Copy A below. Prepare a rough layout of the best design. The paper size should be $3\frac{1}{4}'' \times 5\frac{1}{2}''$.
2. Design a series of traditional thumbnail layouts of Copy B below. Prepare a rough layout of the best design. The paper size should be $3\frac{1}{4}'' \times 5\frac{1}{2}''$.
3. Set type for both postcards. Pull a newsprint proof, and check for accuracy. Pull three reproduction proofs of each form.
4. Paste both the rough layout and a reproduction proof for each postcard down on a piece of illustration board as shown on the rough layout.
5. Cover the finished paste-up with a protective cover.

Supplementary Readings

Polk: *The Practice of Printing*, Chap. 26 (The Principle of Balance)
Turnbull: *The Graphics of Communication*, Chap. 10 (Principles of Layout and Design)
Arnold: *Ink on Paper*, Chap. 19 (Layout)
Ballinger: *Layout*

COPY A

MODERN HIGH SPEED PRINTING DEMANDS...
ultra new printing techniques and
precision craftsmanship.

Our printing firm strives to produce the most modern printing on
high-speed printing equipment. Our
entire operation is geared to quality, high-speed production.

YOUR COMPANY NAME
YOUR ADDRESS
YOUR PHONE NUMBER

COPY B

SLOWLY...
Over the centuries the art of
printing has evolved, being developed
and enriched by famous printers such
as Franklin, Bodoni, Caslon and
Gutenberg.

All work produced in our printing
shop is produced under the same slow,
careful methods. If necessary we
will set type by hand to create a
careful, unhurried, fine piece of
printing.

WITH TIME COMES QUALITY...WE TAKE
THE TIME
Mail us a sample of a letterhead or
other piece, so that we may study it,
and suggest how to perfect it so that
it will rank with work produced by
the masters of the past.
YOUR NAME PRINTING CO.
Your address and telephone number
YOUR COMPANY NAME
Your address and telephone

Modern Layout

Reproduction proof

Traditional Layout

Reproduction proof

Modern Layout rough

Traditional Layout rough

Exploratory Exercise   1

The interested and advanced student can gain more skill by pasting up additional letterheads, matching envelopes and business cards. If typesetting equipment is not available, the student can find compatible types in magazines—both in the text and the advertisements. It is advisable for the student to search through more than one magazine (as well as more than one issue of the same magazine) to find the right typeface for the job. Remember that the type styles should be harmonious with the nature of the firms.

Some suggested copy is given below. Find type which matches your conception of these firms.

```
Faster Movers, local and long
   distance hauling
1234 Service Street
New York, New York


Aero-Space Equipment Company
4321 Smith Street
Houston, Texas


Luxury Furniture
555 North Coal Street
Pittsburgh, Pennsylvania
```

This copy is only a suggestion. The student should not feel bound by it. You can, of course, substitute other copy. If typesetting equipment is available, you may want to design letterheads for a local firm or service organization.

With this exercise, as with all the exercises in this book, it is best to make a small, rough layout of each job *before* beginning the paste-up. You may want to keep the sketches as well as the finished paste-up in your portfolio.

Exploratory Exercise   2

The advanced student will find it interesting to study the results of duplicating already-screened photographs. First, collect a number of examples of halftones from newspapers and magazines. If possible, use one of the printing journals, such as *Graphic Arts Monthly, Inland Printer and American Lithographer* or *Book Production Magazine;* these journals usually contain advertisements which feature a variety of halftone screen rulings.

Next, paste the halftones side by side. Using a magnifying glass, you can rank them from coarsest to finest. When this is done, photograph the already-screened halftones without screening—same size. Next, shoot the same set of halftones half size. Develop these negatives, make prints and compare them with the originals.

With the same set of original halftones, use a screen and repeat the process as above.

If you wish you may mount the finished products and do a paste-up display of these re-screened and unscreened halftone prints.

If platemaking material is available to you, you may wish to have a plate made. A proof pulled from this plate will also make an interesting display.

Exploratory Exercise   3

You may wish to gain practice using proofreaders' marks in the following exercise.

Select a newspaper column about 8″ long. (It should contain at least four paragraphs.) Paste this up, with an overlay sheet. Proceed to mark the following changes in the column you have pasted down:

1. Indicate the entire second paragraph is to be set in bold face type.
2. Remove the third word in the first paragraph.
3. Transpose the last two words in the first paragraph.
4. Mark two or three sentences which are to be set in italic. (You may choose any you like.)

Exploratory Exercise   4

Many elementary design students begin their study by working with masses of black and white. The interested and advanced student may want to try his hand at abstract design, while exploring the point system. For this exercise, you will need a line gauge, a sheet of black construction paper, a piece of illustration board 11″ × 14″ and paper and pencil.

An abstract mass of black paper possesses many design elements. Among these size, shape, proportion and white space surrounding it are within the control of the designer. Make a rough layout of a design using six masses of black paper. These should all be various shapes of squares and rectangles. Vary the sizes, shapes, proportions and placement of these elements to create an interesting design.

When you have completed the design, cut pieces of black construction paper and paste these down in an 8½″ × 11″ area. You may move and adjust the position of each to achieve the design effect you desire. Finally measure the size, in points and picas, of each area of black paper. Mark these down in the margins near each, using sky blue pencil. Save this paste-up for your portfolio.

Exploratory Exercise 5

The interested and advanced student may want to explore this factor further in legibility. Search through magazines to find type styles which are used in display headings of advertisements. Try to get a sampling of words of the same size—but of different faces.

Make a paste-up ranking these different faces according to legibility. When you have completed the paste-up, place an overlay on the paste-up. On this overlay, briefly describe the uses which these typefaces might find in display advertising.

Exploratory Exercise 6

Complete the exercise shown here in order to develop your ability to recognize and visualize common type sizes. Remove a full page display advertisement from a magazine. Paste it down on a piece of 11″ × 14″ illustration board. Attach an overlay sheet. Mark the type sizes of each different face on the overlay. Refer to the study chart in this book frequently for comparison.

Practice at pasting up and labeling the type size of three or four additional advertisements will improve the student's ability to distinguish various type sizes.

Exploratory Exercise 7

The interested and advanced student may enjoy doing a layout of a food label. Every food product canned must at the very least be identified. Almost all manufacturers of processed foods also identify themselves on the packages which contain the food. Canned and processed food producers are among the largest users of printing. The student may use the copy below for his layout. Make several thumbnail sketches before completing the rough layout.

Assume that this label will fit around a number 2 can. Measure a number 2 can with a tape measure and make your final rough same size. If you wish, you may redesign the layout from any label you see in your local grocery store.

```
Scruffy Dog Food, for dogs that
like meat, processed by Doggy,
Incorporated.
```

Exploratory Exercise 8

Advertising agencies, newspapers, magazines and businesses of all kinds use paste-up artists to help sell the products of the nation. The interested and advanced student may want to use his paste-up skills, his Graphic Arts knowledge and ideas in designing an advertisement. Space and its use in an advertisement is of primary importance in presenting the message.

Using the copy below, design an advertisement to fit into a space 14 picas wide and 34 picas deep. If typesetting facilities are not readily available, use Artype or some similar adhesive lettering for your headings and other display elements. Use a standard typewriter for the body copy.

When you have completed the paste-up, try using the same text material in an ad which is 29 picas wide and 34 picas deep. Use a related design and format.

```
     American Tech, Publishers since
1898. Have you seen the latest offer-
ings in Industrial Education texts?
Here is a partial list of new indus-
try-keyed texts now available from
American Tech.  Each has been de-
signed to serve the needs of the
individual student and to meet the
requirements of industry.
American Technical Society's Draft-
     ing, Giachino-Beukema.  This book
     will speed the development of
     skills through the use of meaning-
     ful problems and clear, illustrated
     examples.  $0.00.
Building with Steel, Don A. Halperin.
     Design and construction with steel
     is clarified for engineering stu-
     dents and laymen alike.  A minimum
     of previous experience is required.
     $0.00
Know Your Car, Willard A. Allen.  An
     activity centered presentation of
     the basic principles of automotive
     operation and maintenance.  $0.00
```

Exploratory Exercise 9

Some newspapers, particularly the great metropolitan dailies, have a "brown section" or rotogravure magazine. Copy for rotogravure printing is always pasted up first. Then it is photographed, plates made and the magazine printed. The interested and advanced student will find it profitable to do a paste-up similar to that which is made for a rotogravure section. All gravure copy is screened (both type and pictures) so there is normally no stripping involved in gravure platemaking. Thus, the gravure paste-up may include both halftone and line copy.

First obtain a brief article from any magazine. From some other printed source get halftones and line drawings which you think are appropriate to the subject of the article. The halftones may be from magazines, books or newspapers.

Now make several thumbnails of a page layout. It may be helpful to explore a few rotogravure magazines to suggest some design ideas. Plan to use a page size of 10" by 12". When you have a layout which appeals to you, make outlines in sky blue pencil for the page size, allow 1¼ inch margins at the top and left (for a right hand page) and 1" margins at the bottom and right. Now paste-up the article.

Exploratory Exercise 10

The greeting card industry uses all of the graphic arts processes. Greeting cards use both center layouts and off-center layouts. In general, humorous cards and studio cards use off-center, while religious and more serious cards use formal balance (center layouts). Text for three greeting cards are given below, one of them would be best as an off-center layout, the other two would benefit from a center layout. You may use color in your layout if you wish. If you search through magazines, you can find appropriate cartoon figures or line drawings to use for illustrations. If you are so inclined, you may do your own cartoon figures or line drawings.

Off-center layout: Get well card for the boss.
Page 1 To our Boss!
Page 2 We send a note,
         Instead of a call.
Page 3 A get well greeting,
         From one and all.
Centered layout: Get well card for the boss.

Page 1 To our favorite Boss
Page 2 With hope and cheer,
Page 3 This get well greeting,
         Comes loud and clear.
Centered Layout: Commercial get well card
Page 1 Get well soon
Page 2 Blank or appropriate illustration
Page 3   Sad hands send this message
         Hoping glad news by return
            We hope you'll soon get better
         Your health is our concern
                    SMITH'S PHARMACY

Exploratory Exercise 11

In Project 12 you worked with the front page of a newspaper. For additional practice on this topic you may lay out and paste-up some of the internal pages of a newspaper. Do a page with several photographs, a financial page, a page with several advertisements. Use a 16" × 24" size illustration board.

Exploratory Exercise 12

Many small newspapers and house organs are printed by the offset process. The text material may be set on a typewriter, VariTyper or similar device. The display copy and headlines are often set on a Headliner or similar machine. If such a machine is not available, the artist may have to paste-up the heads, using adhesive lettering. This exercise will develop skills in using adhesive lettering for composing newspaper heads.

Obtain a front page from your local newspaper. Using adhesive lettering, compose the heads listed below. Paste all of the finished work on an 11" × 14" piece of illustration board, and save it for your portfolio.

Select the following heads to be set (you may make substitutions if these are not available on the page.)
a. Two line, one column
b. Three line, one column
c. One line, two column
d. Two line, two column
e. Two line, three column
f. One line, four column display banner

Exploratory Exercise 13

Charts and graphs of all kinds are used in magazines, business publications, advertisements and text books. It is often helpful in showing comparisons to use color to point up similarities and differences. The interested and advanced student may find it profitable and interesting to do a paste-up of a bar graph showing the won-lost record of the major league baseball teams.

Make a thumbnail sketch of your bar-graph first, then do a rough layout. Following your rough layout make the lost record of each team in black, then make a rubylith overlay of the won record. Mark the illustrations board "Black" and the rubylith overlay "Color." Use register marks to indicate how the color and black fit together.

When you have completed the bars of your graph, use adhesive lettering for the team names. Also provide a key to the graph somewhere in your layout.

Exploratory Exercise 14

Many of the techniques used in correcting typewritten composition may be used to correct other forms of copy. The interested student who has gained some of the skills suggested in Project 15 may want to try correcting some of these. Corrections are not too difficult, if the lessons shown in Project 15 were typed on an elite or standard pica machine. Since all letters and numbers are of the same width, direct substitutions may be easily made.

Repeat the lesson, using an IBM *Executive* typewriter for composition. Corrections may be a little more difficult, since the machine uses proportional letter spacing. Note for example, that the lower case "m" is much wider than the lower case "l."

If hot metal composition facilities are available, again repeat the lesson. Set the copy, and the alterations indicated, and pull two sets of reproduction proofs. Make the same corrections outlined in the lesson.

Exploratory Exercise 15

Mail order houses and large department stores which maintain mail order departments issue catalogs for various geographical areas. The catalog staff of these firms often find that they can save the company money by using some pages over and over again. Often the only changes on these pages are changes in the prices. The interested and advanced

student may revise one of these pages. Obtain a Sears and Roebuck or Montgomery Ward catalog and revise one of the pages, by increasing the prices 10% on the items which are offered for sale.

If typesetting facilities are available, have type set to match the face used for these prices.

If typesetting facilities are not available, then you can use adhesive letters for the new prices.

Be sure the catalog page you choose is printed in a paper and ink color which can be reproduced on the camera.

Exploratory Exercise 16

One of the most common promotional devices used by every kind of industry is the calendar. Wall calendars, wallet calendars, desk calendars and pocket daily calendars are distributed free to business people all over the country. Banks, automobile dealers, drug stores and businesses of all sorts use these daily reminders to keep their name before the potential customer. The interested and advanced student will find many alternate uses for tint screens in designing and pasting up a date folder for one month of the year. The necessary type for this project may be either adhesive lettering or a reproduction proof, the tint screens may be used for a border strip along the top and bottom of the folder. A thumbnail sketch is shown below. Execute a rough layout and finished paste-up for the thumbnail sketch shown below.

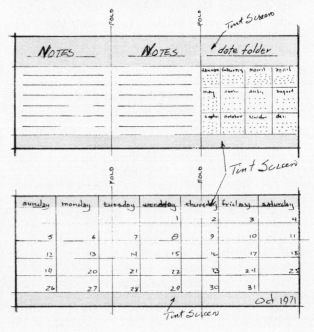

146

Exploratory Exercise   17

This lesson has explored some of the uses of the ruling pen to produce solids, rectangles and rules of varying widths. The standard ruling pen is limited to straight lines. The interested and advanced student who would like to gain more skill may wish to complete the exercises below.

A bow compass and ruling pen may be purchased which will rule circles of various sizes. Essentially this device consists of a standard ruling pen, mounted on a compass. The serious paste-up artist will want to own one of these pens. Thus he can rule circles of any size, including outline circles and rectangles with rounded corners. All of these display elements may be used creatively in advertising paste-ups.

Rule the following design elements, and mount them on a piece of 11″ × 14″ illustration board.

    a. 1″ solid circle (Rule a 3 point perimeter and fill in the center using a #2 sable brush and India ink.)

    b. 2″ solid circle

    c. 3″ solid circle

    d. 2″ outline circle (leave the center of the circle with a 1″ uninked circle.)

    e. 3″ outline circle, with a 1″ spot in center

    f. 2″ square solid, with rounded corners

    g. 2″ × 4″ solid rectangle, with rounded corners

    h. 3″ × 4″ outline rectangle, with rounded corners

Exploratory Exercise   18

The ambitious student may gain additional practice in the use of a ruling pen and in other paste-up skills by executing another rough layout and finished paste-up of a business form. A rough layout of a requisition is shown below. Use a Vari Typer or standard typewriter for necessary copy.

Exploratory Exercise   19

Internal house organs and sales letters are often composed on the typewriter. The finished appearance may be improved if these publications and letters are justified on both margins. The advanced and interested student may find it profitable to justify the copy shown below.

```
Dear Friend:
Want to earn more money? -- a lot
more?
Well, here's your opportunity ...
You see, we train men for America's
largest and fastest growing indus-
tries, without interfering with their
present jobs.

The demand for TRAINED men is TRE-
MENDOUS.  Thousands of replacements
are needed each year, in addition to
the thousands upon thousands of new
jobs created by the increased activ-
ity in business and industry.

The man who can qualify and does make
the grade can say good-by to a dull,
routine job and a pay check that is
much too small to meet the high cost
of living today.

If you are between 18 and 50, return
the enclosed card today.  Do it
promptly, and we shall send to you a
free SELF-ANALYSIS JOB PREFERENCE
TEST.  Mail the card TODAY.

            Sincerely yours,
```

Exploratory Exercise   20

Banks and other firms customarily issue an annual report. These reports inform the investors of the companies' progress and of their earnings. Annual reports often include a table which briefly describes and summarizes the report. The interested and advanced student may gain further experience in layout and paste-up skills by executing a thumbnail sketch, a rough layout and a completed paste-up for the table for an annual report. A thumbnail sketch of the report is provided below. Copy for the table is shown immediately below the thumbnail sketch.

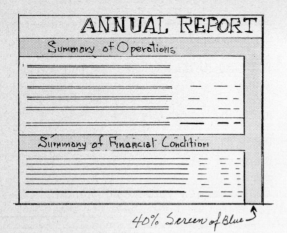

40% Screen of Blue

COPY: ANNUAL REPORT

Summary of Operations

Net Sales	$158,000	$124,000	$106,000
Income before federal			
income taxes	7,600	6,241	3,770
Income taxes	3,043	3,221	1,836
Net income	4,567	3,020	1,834
Net income per share	$1.08	$0.96	$0.73

Summary of Financial Condition

Current assets	82,000	63,000	55,000
Current liabilities	16,021	12,243	10,991
Working capital	65,979	40,777	14,009
Net plant account	29,036	20,042	15,001
Retained earnings	4,006	2,091	7,004
Common stock			
earnings	25,030	17,351	7,995

Exploratory Exercise   21

The discerning student may find the following lesson of help in comparing the quality of cold-type versus hot metal composition. Obtain a news story from your local newspaper, printed letterpress. Paste this down on the left hand side of an 11″ × 14″ piece of illustration board. Using a strike-on letter, or similar cold-type device, compose the same copy found in the news story. Make every effort to duplicate the spacing, line width, type style and format found in the letterpress copy. Mount your cold-type copy on the right hand portion of the illustration board.

Answer the following questions related to composition:

1. Which composition method achieves the best horizontal alignment of characters on the line?

2. Which method creates the most pleasing and uniform word spacing?
3. Would a photocomposed or a strike-on cold-type method compare most favorably with the hot metal composition?
4. Which column would be easier to make corrections in?
5. If the type form were available, which method would be easiest to make duplicate proofs? Corrections? Deletions? Additions?
6. Which method is best suited for an economical publication?

Exploratory Exercise   22

Local clubs, service organizations and trade or manufacturing organizations often put out newsletters, bulletins and small magazines or journals. When these organizations are small or have small promotional budgets, they will probably produce their literature using cold-type composition.

The interested and advanced student will find it profitable and interesting to compose some copy for a page from a limited circulation journal using a headline writing device and a VariTyper. When he has the text, he should execute a finished paste-up for his portfolio. A rough layout of the page is provided. The text copy for this project is given immediately below the layout.

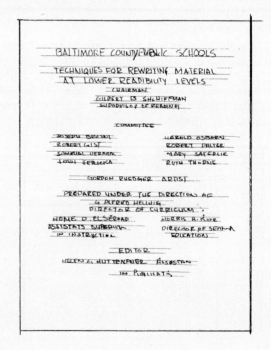

Exploratory Exercise 23

The student who wants to gain more understanding and practice handling various halftones may paste-up the following pieces of artwork:

1. Prepare a paste-up with a square inset photograph. Prepare another with a round inset photograph.

2. Prepare a paste-up, using a display line overprinted on top of an illustration.

3. Prepare an illustration to be printed in outline form. Mount the illustration (either a photograph or a printed halftone) and outline the subject, using opaque white paint.

4. Prepare a vignette halftone. You will need an air brush to feather the image into the background.

5. A highlight halftone may be made by painting out highlight portions of the illustration.

Exploratory Exercise 24

Specially designed matchbook covers are widely used promotional devices. Many firms, such as insurance agencies distribute books of matches to keep the name of the agency before the public. Often the match book will have a snapshot of one of the salesmen on the cover.

The interested and advanced student may gain experience in layout as well as the handling of photographs by making a thumbnail sketch, a rough layout and a finished paste-up for a matchbook cover. Copy for the paste-up is supplied below. Because the matchbook cover is $1\frac{1}{2}''$ wide and $4\frac{1}{2}''$ long, it will be best to do the finished paste-up "twice up" ($3''$ wide and $9''$ long). Use a snapshot of one of your friends as an illustration. Crop the photograph so that only the head is used in the finished product. When you have completed the paste-up, write "reduce to 50% outside the margin.

Complete Coverage Agency, insurance of all kinds —life, auto, real estate, commercial, health and accident.
Mr. Robert X. Donee, agent.

Exploratory Exercise 25

To gain more practice in scaling illustrations and copy, complete the exercises suggested here, and write the answers on a sheet of paper. Record both original size, new size and reduction percentage, where possible.

a. What would be the size of the front page, from your local newspaper, if it were reduced to 62% of its present size? What would be the width of the columns, in picas?

b. What would be the width in picas, of this line of type, if this page were blown up to $12''$ wide?

c. What would be the new depth of this page, in picas, if the page were reduced to 80% of its present size?

d. What would be the new width of this page, in picas, if it were blown up to 140% of its present size?

Exploratory Exercise 26

The testimonial is a commonly used form of advertising support. These testimonials often include a head shot of the person who is quoted in the advertisement. The interested and advance student will find it profitable to do a paste-up for such an advertisement. A rough layout of a typical testimonial is given below. The text matter for the ad is given immediately below the thumbnail sketch. The advertisement will appear in a magazine occu-

149

pying a space 10 picas wide and 15 picas deep. Your paste-up should be done at least twice up and marked for reduction. Use a photograph of one of your friends and crop it to show only the head. Mark the photograph for reduction to fit in the block window you have provided in the paste-up. Mount the photograph next to the line art, on the illustration board.

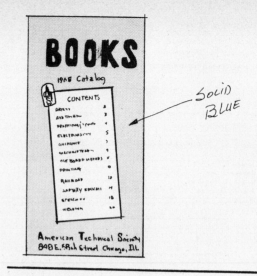

$636

WHILE LEARNING

and I used the money to outfit a complete shop. Now I earn more than $3.25 per hour in my spare time.

                    Friend's Name
                    your town, your state

Exploratory Exercise   27

Study the color wheel. Answer the questions below. Place the answers at the bottom center of the overlay sheet.
   a. What is the complementary color of violet?
   b. What are the triadic colors associated with orange?
   c. What are the monochromatic colors closely associated with green?
   d. List four cold colors.
   e. List four warm colors.

Exploratory Exercise   28

The interested and advanced student who has been doing these exploratory exercises regularly will find it useful to go back through his portfolio to find those exercises which used color overlays. Register marks should be added to those exercises, so that the position of the color in relation to the black is correctly indicated.

Exploratory Exercise   29

Color lends interest and gains attention to advertisements. The interested and advanced student will gain additional experience in the use of color in layouts by executing a finished paste-up for the rough layout shown below.

Exploratory Exercise   30

Blocks of color are often used in display advertising, to lend interest and to gain attention. Below is a rough layout for an advertisement to be used by a consulting firm. The interested and advanced student will gain additional experience in handling opaque colors by executing a finished paste-up following this rough layout. Use simple line drawings where indicated on the rough layout. Register marks should be used to show the proper relationship between the color overlays and the black and white part of the illustration.

NOTE: *Opaque* colors are rarely used in offset printing, but they are very common in screen process printing. The paste-up artist will follow the same procedures in a paste-up for silk screen.

Exploratory Exercise   31

A number of interesting effects can be obtained by over-printing transparent inks. The interested and advanced student may find it profitable to gain further experience in handling transparent colors by executing several finished paste-ups from the following rough layout. Each time he will want to vary the colors used. (If equipment is available, you may wish to have the various exercises printed. If two color processes are not available, the student may use Bourges Colotone for his color paste-ups.)

Text matter for the project should be in black; it may be done with adhesive lettering.

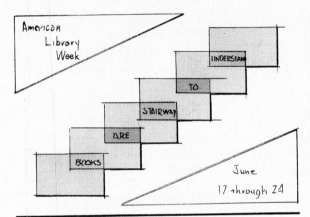

Exploratory Exercise   32

Using the triangle below, see how many different colors you can make by combining the three primary transparent colors. Use Bourges transparent color overlays. You may want to try this several times.

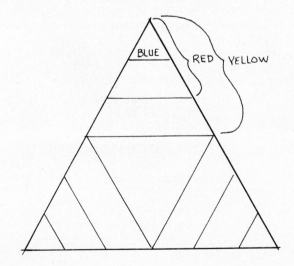

Exploratory Exercise   33

The principle employed in the imitation duotone may be used to great advantage by the paste-up artist. Background colors, shading and contrasting effect may be easily obtained, in addition to the usual duotone effect. Here are a few examples which may be incorporated into a single paste-up by the interested student.

a. Place a line drawing on the overlay, with a solid color on the board.

b. Place a textured area on the board and a line drawing on the overlay.

c. Place some copy printed in reverse on the overlay, and a solid on the board.

d. Place a different texture or screen tint values on the overlay and the board.

Exploratory Exercise   34

Using the facilities available, plan layouts for, and paste-ups of, various greeting cards that you have occasion to use during the year. Use color on some, if possible, and select the typefaces to suit the sentiment to be expressed. Relate your choice of color of ink, finish and color of paper and message into an integrated design.

Source List
of Paste-Up Equipment

Adhesive Lettering and Tapes

Ad Lettering
7380 Beverly Blvd.
L. A., Calif. 90036

Artype, Inc.
345 E. Terra Cotta Ave.
Crystal Lake, Ill. 60014

Cello-Tak Lettering Corp.
131 W. 45th Street
New York, N. Y. 10036

Chart-Pak, Inc.
One River Road
Leeds, Mass. 01053

Fototype, Inc.
1414 Roscoe St.
Chicago, Ill. 60657
and
2883 E. La Palma
Anaheim, Calif. 92806

Para-tone, Inc.
P.O. Box 645
Countryside, Ill. 60525

Underwood Supply Co. Div.
(Montroy Supply Co.)
4165 Beverly Blvd.
L. A., Calif. 90004

Brushes and Inks

Bruning, Charles Co.
1800 W. Central Road
Mount Prospect, Ill. 60056

Carter's Ink Co.
239 First
Cambridge, Mass. 02141

M. Grumbacher, Inc.
460 W. 34th Street
New York, N.Y. 10001

Winsor & Newton, Inc.
555 Winsor Drive
Secaucus, N. J. 07094

Drawing Equipment

Alteneder, Theo. and Sons
1225 Spring Garden St.
Philadelphia, Pa. 19123

Bruning, Charles Co.
1800 W. Central Rd.
Mount Prospect, Ill. 60056

Carter's Ink Co.
239 First
Cambridge, Mass. 02141

Dietzgen, Eugene, Co.
2425 No. Sheffield Ave.
Chicago, Ill. 60614

Gramercy Guild Group, Inc.
1145A W. Custer Place
Denver, Colorado 80223

Keuffel and Esser Co.
Whippany Road
Morristown, N. J. 07960

National Card Mat & Board Co.
4318 Carroll Ave.
Chicago, Ill. 60624
and
14455 Don Julian Road
City of Industry, Calif. 91746

Lettering Equipment and Guides

Hunt Mfg. Co.
1405 Locust Street
Philadelphia, Pa. 19102
(Speedball pens)

Dietzgen, Eugene, Co.
2425 N. Sheffield Ave.
Chicago, Ill. 60614

Keuffel and Esser Co.
Whippany Road
Morristown, N. J. 07960

Letterguide Co.
4247 O St.
Lincoln, Neb. 68503

Wood- Regan Instrument Co.
Nutley, N. J. 07110
(Wrico lettering pen)

Photocomposition and Cold Type

Filmotype
7500 McCormick Blvd.
Skokie, Ill. 60076

Photo Typositor, Inc.
305 E. 46th St.
New York, N. Y. 10017

Striprinter, Inc.
21 N. W. 41st Street
Oklahoma City, Oklahoma 73118

Ulano Graphic Arts Supplies, Inc.
210 E. 86th St.
New York, N.Y. 10028

VariTyper Corp.
11 Mt. Pleasant Ave.
Hanover, N. J. 07936

Proof Presses and Supplies

Vandercook & Sons, Inc.
3601 W. Touhy Ave.
Chicago, Ill. 60645

Rules

Gaebel Steel Rulers
102 Ball Street
E. Syracuse, N. Y. 13057

Wax Coating Devices

Lectro-Stick Co.
3721 N. Broadway
Chicago, Ill. 60640

Schaefer Machine Co., Inc.
Boston Post Rd.
Clinton, Conn. 06413

Bibliography

Graphic Arts
Paste-Up

Arnold, Edmund C. *Ink on Paper 2.* New York: Harper and Row, 1972, 374 pages.

Ballinger, Raymond A., *Layout,* New York: Reinhold Publishing Corp. 1970, 96 pages.

Basic Photography for the Graphic Arts, Rochester: Eastman Kodak, 1970, 45 pages.

Carlsen, Darvey E. *Graphic Arts.* Peoria: Charles A. Bennett Co., 1970, 208 pages.

Cleeton, G. U., Pitkin, C. W. and Cornwell, Raymond L. *General Printing.* Bloomington, Illinois: McKnight & McKnight, 1963, 203 pages.

Cogoli, John E., *Photo-Offset Fundamentals.* Bloomington, Illinois: McKnight & McKnight, 1967, 384 pages.

Karch, R. Randolph, *Graphic Arts Procedures— Basic.* Chicago: American Technical Society, 1970, 409 pages.

Karch, R. Randolph and Buber, E. J. *Graphic Arts Procedures — The Offset Processes.* Chicago: American Technical Society, 1967, 570 pages.

Lithographer 3 & 2, Washington, D. C.: Government Printing Office, 1963, 503 pages.

Polk, R. W. & Polk, E. W. *The Practice of Printing.* Peoria: Charles A. Bennett Co., 1971, 328 pages.

Sayre, I. H., *Photography and Platemaking for Photo-Lithography.* Chicago: Lithographic Textbook Co., 1969, 464 pages.

Silver, Gerald A., *Printing Estimating.* Chicago: American Technical Society, 1970, 156 pages.

Theory and Practice of Lithography. Washington, D.C.: Government Printing Office, 1964, 109 pages.

Turnbull, A. T. & Baird, R. N., *The Graphics of Communication.* New York: Holt, Rinehart and Winston, 1968, 395 pages.

Glossary

Acetate. A flexible plastic material for making overlays on paste-ups; can be transparent or translucent.

Agate. A printer's unit of measure equal to 5½ points, or about 1/13 of an inch. Chiefly used in measuring composition for classified advertising.

Air Brush. A small, hand-held spray gun which applies paint by means of compressed air.

Antique. A rough textured paper.

Ascender. The portion of a letter which projects above the body of the letter. The letters l, k, b and d have ascenders.

Artwork. All of the material, illustrations and paste-ups, related to a particular printing job collectively.

Axis. An imaginary, or real line through a layout upon which copy may be aligned or related or symmetrically arranged.

Bearers. Heavy rules or borders placed around a type form before proofing to protect delicate serifs and yield evenly inked impressions.

Ben Day Screen. A pattern placed over artwork to create a tint, texture or screen effect.

Blanket. A sheet of rubber wrapped around a metal cylinder on an offset press. The inked image is transferred from the lithographic plate to the blanket and then to the sheet of paper.

Bleed. Copy, drawings and illustrations which run off the edge of a printed sheet.

Blow-up. An enlarged or magnified print made from a piece of copy.

Blue Line Proof. A photographic proof made from a lithographic negative on a paper producing a blue image; also called a "blueprint."

Boldface. An alternate typeface, heavier and darker than the standard; used for emphasis.

Bond Paper. A medium weight paper that has been sized to accept ink; used for stationery and business forms.

Brown Line Proof. A photographic proof made from a lithographic negative on a paper producing a brown image; also called a brownprint.

Burnish. To cause adhesive material to adhere to artwork by rubbing with a blunt instrument.

Camera-Ready Copy. Proofs, drawings, typing and any other artwork supplied to the printer in a finished form, ready for photographing; also called "camera copy."

Caps and Lower Case. Capital and small letters used together, sometimes abbreviated to C & lc.

Caps and Small Caps. Large and small capital letters used together.

Caption. The copy set above or below a photograph or illustration.

Center Balance. A layout theory in which all elements of the copy are balanced on an optical axis that runs down the center of the page. Often called formal or symmetrical balance.

Chroma. A measure of the intensity or saturation of a color, e.g. *bright* red, or *dull* green.

Coated Paper. A glossy, smooth finished paper that has been coated with a thin layer of clay or similar substance.

Cold Type. Composition produced by photographic, strike-on, typewriter or similar means other than hot metal or foundry type.

Color Key Proof. A proof made on film yielding an image in a color approximating that chosen for the job.

Color Wheel. A circular pattern with the colors of the spectrum arranged in their related order.

Compass. A drafting instrument for ruling accurate circles.

Comprehensive Layout. A careful drawing of a proposed piece of printing, to the same size, color and detail of the finished job.

Contact Print. A print, the same size as the negative made on a photosensitive paper.

Continuous Tone Copy. Wash drawings, photographs and similar pieces of artwork where the transition of tone from light to dark is gradual.

Continuous Tone Negative. A film negative of continuous tone copy in which the gradual values of gray have been reproduced, but reversed.

Copy Preparation. Assembling, editing and marking-up the elements of a job for typesetting or paste-up.

Counter. A closed-in area in a letter, for instance, o, e, d and b contain counters.

Crop. To mark an illustration or photograph to indicate what portion of it is to be reproduced.

Cross-Rule Form. A printed form having both vertical and horizontal lines which intersect.

Cut. A letterpress printing plate in which the non-image areas have been etched below the surface.

Descenders. The portion of a letter which projects below the body of the letter. The letters y, g, j, and p have descenders.

Display Line. A line of large type, such as a newspaper headline.

Dividers. A drafting instrument used for marking off a series of uniform spaces.

Drafting Machine. A device which serves as a T square and triangle.

Drawing Board. An accurately manufactured piece of softwood, trimmed square on all sides. Used for mounting the illustration board used for a paste-up.

Dropout Halftone. A halftone plate in which the dots in the highlight portions have been removed.

Dummy. A working drawing with illustrations sketched in and copy indicated, showing size, page order and arrangement of a proposed printing job.

Duotone. A halftone made by printing two images of the same illustration one over the other, using different color of ink each time.

Ears. Small blocks of copy set on both sides of the nameplate of a newspaper.

Em. A unit of printer's measure, equal to the square of the type size with which he is working.

En. A unit of printer's measure, equal to half of an em.

Engraving. A letterpress printing plate in which the non-image areas have been etched below the surface. Sometimes called a cut.

Filter. A thin sheet of colored glass or gelatin inserted between the camera lens and copy. Filters are used to accentuate or drop out selected colors from the copy.

Fixative. A spray applied to drawings to make them permanent.

Flats. Large sheets of colored masking paper which support film negatives or positives in position for platemaking.

Flush Left. All lines of copy aligned along the left margin.

Flush Right. All lines of copy aligned along the right margin.

Folio. The page number.

Font. The full alphabet in capital and lower case letters along with numbers and selected symbols for a single style and size of type.

Galley. A shallow, metal tray used by printers to store type and type forms.

Galley Proof. A proof from type before it is spaced out into pages.

Gang. To group together two or more jobs on a single press run.

Geometric Center. The precise mechanical center of the page.

Gravure Printing. Printing produced from plates in which the image is etched below the surface.

Hairline. A printer's rule, finer than one point in width.

Halftone Negative. A film negative of continuous tone copy in which the gradual values of gray have been reproduced as discrete dots of black or white.

Headliner. A device producing display lines of type photographically on strips of film or print paper.

High Contrast Film. Film which reproduces copy as dense black or not at all.

Highlight. The whitest part of a photograph.

Highlight Halftone. A halftone in which all dots have been removed from the highlight portions in order to increase the contrast and sparkle.

Hot Metal Composition. Printing produced from metal type cast from a mold.

Hue. The name of any color, e.g., red, blue, green.

IBM Composer (Free Standing). A small desk-top direct image cold type composing machine, which prints letter images from a rapidly moving round type element. The machine is about the size of a "Selectric" typewriter.

IBM Magnetic Tape "Selectric" Composer (MT/SC). A tape driven, direct image cold type composing machine which prints letter images from a rapidly moving, round type element. Machine stores keystrokes on reel of magnetic tape.

Illustration Board. A heavy, durable cardboard on which paste-ups are made.

Image Guidelines. A set of lines drawn in light blue pencil on paste-up to mark the area in which the printed image will be contained.

Impression. The pressure applied to the sheet of paper by the form; the printed paper itself.

India Ink. A dense opaque black ink, principally used for ruling and line drawings.

Inset Halftone. An illustration containing a smaller illustration within its borders showing a magnified detail.

Insert. A special page or signature (group of pages) bound into a publication.

Italic Type. A slanted close-fitting style of type.

Job Proof. A proof of type after it has been spaced out in page form.

Justification. The spacing out of a line of type so that it will be aligned along both the right and left margins. The usual newspaper column is an example of justified composition.

Key Plate. In multicolor offset printing, the base plate to which the other plates are positioned. It usually contains the bulk of the copy and artwork, and is usually the black ink plate.

Layout. A sketch or drawing by which the designer shows his conception of the finished printed page.

Lead. A strip of printer's spacing material 2 points or approximately 1/36 of an inch wide.

Letterpress Printing. Printing produced from type or plates in which the image is raised from the form.

Letterspace. The addition of extra space between letters in a line to add width to the line or to improve its appearance.

Light Table. A table with a glass top, lighted from below. Used for stripping negatives into a flat.

Line Copy. Drawings, type proofs, typewriter copy and similar pieces of artwork that are black and white, without shades of gray.

Line Gauge. A printer's scale; sometimes called a type rule, type gauge, or line measure.

Lithographic Printing. Printing produced from plates in which the image is formed on the surface of a plate. The ink adheres only to the image areas.

Logotype. A trade design or emblem of a company or its product.

Mask. A piece of paper or plastic used to cover unwanted areas of a photograph, etc. Also, a film negative or positive designed to increase or decrease contrast or adjust color balance.

Middletones. The medium tones comprising the range between the highlights and the shadows in a photograph or halftone illustration.

Moire. An unwanted interference pattern sometimes formed when two screens are placed over one another; similar to a "watered silk" pattern in some fabrics.

Monochromatic Film. A color blind film used for copying black and white copy.

Mortise. An opening in a photoengraving, cut out so that type may be inserted.

Nameplate. A display insignia usually found at the top of a newspaper, bearing its name.

Negative. A photographic film in which all elements of the original copy are rendered in reverse.

Negative Space. The white space, or unprinted area of a page.

Newsprint. The paper stock on which most newspapers are printed.

Nonpareil. A printer's unit of measure, approximately equal to 1/12 of an inch; one nonpareil equals 6 points.

Off-Center Balance. A layout theory in which the design elements are *not* symmetrically grouped around the axis of the page. It is often called asymmetrical, modern or contemporary balance.

Offset Printing. Lithographic printing produced from plates in which the image has been transferred from a plate to a rubber blanket and then to the sheet of paper.

Opaque Ink. An ink which does not permit any color over which it is printed to show through.

Opaquing. The hand operation of painting over small imperfections in negatives with a light-stopping paint.

Open Window Negative. A negative with a transparent opening in it produced by photographing a black area on the camera copy. This is done to provide a place for halftones.

Optical Center. A point on a page, pleasing to the eye, above the mechanical center of the page.

Orthochromatic Film. A film used for copying black and white originals that does not pick up blue guidelines.

Outline Halftone. A halftone finish in which the dot pattern stops at the edge of the subject.

Overlay. A sheet of acetate, tracing paper or similar material placed over a paste-up to hold copy that will appear in another color or for special instructions on the job.

Overprint Halftone. A halftone finish in which line copy has been exposed over a halftone; sometimes called a surprint.

Panchromatic Film. A film sensitive to all colors; used for reproducing multicolored copy.

Paper Guidelines. A set of lines drawn in light blue pencil on a paste-up to mark the outside edge of the sheet of paper to be used for the job.

Paste-up. A composite group of proofs, drawings and artwork mounted on illustration board for photographic reproduction.

Photoengraving. A letterpress printing plate in which the non-image areas have been etched below the surface. Sometimes called a cut, or engraving.

Pica. A printer's unit of measure, approximately equal to 1/6 of an inch. 1 pica equals 12 points, 6 picas equal 1 inch.

Plugging. The filling in with ink of open portions in or around letters or between dots in a halftone.

Point. A printer's unit of measure, approximately equal to 1/72 of an inch. 1 pica equals 12 points, 1 slug equals 6 points and 1 lead equals 2 points.

Positive. A print in which all copy is rendered in the same value and density as the original. The opposite of a negative.

Press Proof. A print made by using the actual press, inks and paper planned for the finished run.

Primary Colors. The colors of the visual spectrum: red, green and blue-violet; the ink or pigment colors: red, yellow and blue.

Print Trimmer. A hand operated cutting board used to trim proofs and illustrations.

Projection Print. An enlargement or reduction print made by printing a negative with a photographic enlarger.

Register Marks. Special marks resembling crosses placed in the margin of the paste-up to provide a point of reference to position overlays for color plates.

Reverse Print. A print made of copy in which the colors are the opposite of the original. White lettering would appear on a black background in the print if the copy had black lettering on a white background; a "negative" print.

Revised Proofs. A set of proofs pulled to show corrections made on a previous set of proofs.

Roman Type. A classical style type, created by early printers, possessing heavy and light strokes and terminating with serifs.

Rough Layout. A drawing, usually done in charcoal pencil, of a proposed piece of printing. Its function is to show space relationships and major copy elements.

Rubylith® Film. A hand cut stencil film used on artwork to make solids and to mask or outline images.

Rule. A line on a page, or the strip of metal used to print a rule in letterpress.

Ruling Pen. A drafting instrument designed to produce neat, uniform lines or rules.

Sans Serif Type. A type style which possesses no serifs; where the terminal strokes of the letters end without a crossline.

Scribing. The removal by hand of the emulsion on a negative to allow light to come through.

Script Type. A cursive type which resembles hand written letters; used for contrast with Roman type.

Secondary Colors. A color produced by blending two primary colors.

Serifs. Finishing strokes on certain letters; also called crosslines or feet.

Shadow. The darkest tones in a photograph. In a halftone a shadow is usually covered by a 90% or 95% dot.

Silk Screen Printing. A printing process in which the image is cut into a stencil that is supported by silk, nylon or some other screen material. The ink is forced through the openings in the screen to the object being printed upon.

Size. To treat the surface of paper so that it will accept ink.

Slug. A strip of printer's spacing material approximately equal to 1/12 of an inch; 2 slugs equal 1 pica.

Small Caps. A smaller size of capital letters that is the height of the body of the lower case letters in the font.

Speedball Pen. A special pen for which tips can be obtained in a variety of line widths and styles.

Square Serif Type. A class of typefaces in which most of the major strokes of the letter terminate in square crosslines of uniform thickness.

Stripping. The operation of combining halftone, line and color separation negatives on a flat in the proper position for printing.

Surprint. An overprint in which line copy is superimposed over a halftone.

Text Type. An ornate type style, patterned after the early letter styles found in hand copied manuscripts.

Text Matter. Composition set without ornamentation, usually justified, and used for the mass of body copy.

Text Paper. A rough finish, elegant paper used for fine printing.

Thumbnail Layout. A small, quickly done drawing of a proposed piece of printing. Its function is to provide a means to rapidly explore various design ideas.

Tint Block. A solid panel or area covered by a light or flat color.

Tint Screen. A pattern placed over copy to produce a gray area, or a special textured effect.

Transparency. A photographic positive on a transparent film base.

Transparent Ink. A type of ink which permits the blending of primary colors to obtain secondary colors.

Triangle. A flat, three-sided device used to draw diagonal or vertical lines, usually used with a T square.

Trim Guidelines. A set of lines drawn in light blue pencil on a paste-up to mark the area of paper to be trimmed away.

T Square. A drafting instrument used to align copy in parallel fashion on a paste-up.

Vacuum Frame. A device designed to bring a plate and negative into close contact so that the image can be transferred to the plate without distortion.

Value. The degree of lightness or darkness of a color as *light* brown, or *dark* blue.

VariTyper. A specialized typewriter which will produce a variety of sizes and styles of typing.

Velox. A contact print on photographic paper.

Vignette Halftone. An illustration in which the background around the subject appears to fade away without an abrupt change.

White Space. The unprinted area around the copy or text, sometimes called negative space.

Window. An opening in an overlay, flat or mask, usually left to make room for an illustration.